The Christian Reader's Guide
to the Old Testament

Also by David Waite Yohn
*The Contemporary Preacher and His Task*

# The Christian Reader's Guide
# to the Old Testament

DAVID WAITE YOHN

William B. Eerdmans Publishing Company
Grand Rapids, Michigan

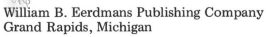

*With respect and
devotion to N.L.W.*

## An Opening Word

The purposes of this book are to provide beginning students and laymen with some basic instruction in the background, form, and content of the Old Testament—with specific interest in the meaning of the concept covenant—and, at the same time, to allow the biblical material to raise and stimulate questions, problems, and issues of contemporary life. It is intended to be instructive (though not technical) and to focus the material covered on the situation of our modern lives.

All of the material is presented in the form of sermons. In the first place, this form builds in certain qualities that make it more understandable for the reader not trained in biblical scholarship. Sermons demand brevity in the presentation of material (thus there are no footnotes, bibliography, or technical discussions), careful selection of the material presented, and application of the material to the situation of modern man. There can be no hiding behind abstract discussions; everything stated must unfold an approach to life. Sermon-making is intensely practical.

There is a second reason I have chosen the sermon form. In this day of the "poverty of the pulpit" we need some new directions in preaching to move it out of its old ways. I tried to address this situation in *The Contemporary Preacher and His Task* (Eerdmans, 1969). I am firmly persuaded that the task of preaching has changed in our churches, and the sermons in this present volume represent for me the nature of that change.

There is no pretense that any of the insights into the

Bible is new, unique, or original. For background I have intentionally depended on only a few works: Oesterley and Robinson, *Hebrew Religion* (S.P.C.K., London, 1952); John Bright, *A History of Israel* (Westminster, Philadelphia, 1959); Bernhard Anderson, *Understanding the Old Testament* (Prentice-Hall, Englewood Cliffs, New Jersey, 1966 edition); Gerhard von Rad, *Old Testament Theology*, Vols. I and II (Harper, New York, 1962 and 1965); Walther Eichrodt, *Theology of the Old Testament*, Vols. I and II (Westminster, Philadelphia, 1961 and 1967). Without apology, but only with the greatest gratitude for such a fine work, I have based the outline for this volume on Eichrodt's first volume. I am indebted to this book especially for much of the technical material.

I hope that many of the approaches to the Old Testament material, the insights, interpretations, and suggestions, present some original and new directions for contemporary churches. I hope that what is said will cause laymen to raise some questions that are new to them. I have been most encouraged by the response that I have received to this material, all of which has been actually preached.

Finally, I quote the words of Origen in *De Principiis*: "These things have occurred to me at present concerning matters so difficult to discuss. If anyone can find better understandings, then let his insights be deemed more helpful."

—David Waite Yohn
*Massachusetts Institute of Technology
Cambridge, Mass.*

Contents

## PART THREE: THE INTERNAL LIFE
## OF THE COMMUNITY

## PART FOUR: THE NATURE OF
## THE COVENANT GOD

## PART FIVE: THE HOPE AND SALVATION
## OF COVENANT LIVING

# Preface

There are three words we must look at first. One of them is *Israel*. Israel is the term for the worshipping community whose God was Yahweh. It was composed mostly of Hebrews, although there were other peoples of the ancient world who also participated in this worshipping community.

*Yahweh* was Israel's God. Transliterated from the Hebrew, the name is written YHWH. There are no vowels in the Hebrew script. A likely reconstruction of the vowel tones yields the name Yahweh (occasionally written Jahweh). Older translations render it "Jehovah."

The final word—which we will be using a great deal—is *covenant*. The covenant binds Yahweh and Israel together. There are five major covenants in the Old Testament. Listed in the historical, linear way they developed, these are: the covenant of Moses, the covenant of David, the covenant of Jeremiah, the covenant of Abraham, and the covenant of Noah. They appear in the text of our Bible in the order: Noah's, Abraham's, Moses', David's, and Jeremiah's.

PART ONE

# THE MEANING OF COVENANT LIFE

# 1. Breaking Open the Covenant Faith

### Genesis 9:8-19

I grew up in a small midwestern town where people had a sense of godliness. They felt themselves to be godly people. In the last half of the twentieth century it is difficult to find such a sense of godliness, is it not? Early in the Old Testament we are told that we are created in the image of God. A little later we read that we are created a little lower than the angels. But as the events of the world rush on, most of us have a sense that the distance between divine and human attributes is widening. A sense of godliness is becoming more and more foreign to our experience.

Jesus counseled us, "Do not be anxious." But we are the most anxious and frenetic and nervous people that ever existed, both in our society and, interestingly enough, in the Christian church. Again, Jesus promised that he would give us peace that passes our understanding. Yet among us there is an increasing recognition of how little understanding we have and how hard peace is to come by, either in our personal lives or in our public lives. Why is this so? The answer given from the Judeo-Christian perspective is that man's covenant relation with God is broken.

For Israel the covenant relation between God and man was the absolutely critical issue. When that relation was intact, men had the peace of God that gave them understanding and insight. They were free from their anxieties and guilt because they trusted in God. They had a vision that gave them an insight into the goal of their lives and the totality of human life. They were endued with a high sense of destiny. But when that covenant relation was out of joint, none of this applied. We must begin, then, by asking what the ingredients of the covenant relationship are. What is it that binds God and man together? What are the elements of this thing called covenant?

The first ingredient of the covenant is this: God reveals himself as a known quantity in the ongoing events of the lives of men. He lets us know himself as a fact in our history. For Israel, Yahweh was not an unknown and intangible thing. Israel was supremely convinced that she had evidence of his person. The Exodus was the supreme moment in her history; and as she reflected back upon this event, she became persuaded that in it she knew Yahweh. There was no question in her mind as to what kind of person God was and is. He releases captives, he resists oppression, he lifts up the downtrodden, and he destroys the oppressor. Israel knew from the events of the Exodus that this was the kind of person her God was and is, and the fact of God became a very personal experience. Today we may accept or reject that perspective, but it is not a point that can be argued. Those who know God personally can faithfully testify to that knowledge. The covenant relation can be demonstrated, but it cannot be debated.

In Israel's faith God was not understood in speculative terms. Israel had no philosophy, no systematic theology, no doctrine. She never could ask the question so familiar in the Western world: "Does God exist?" That would have been like asking "Do I love my family?" or "Is hydrogen the basic stuff of the universe?" It was a given fact. To ask the question "Does God exist?" indicated that the covenant was already broken. Nor could God be learned or taught in the form of a lesson. The church expends a great deal of energy on this enterprise, but Israel made it quite clear that ultimately God can only be demonstrated in the lives of his people.

So Israel understood God as breaking into the lives of people. He had intimate dealings with them. This could be demonstrated in the lives of men like Abraham—or Martin Luther King. He molded men to his will. This could be demonstrated in the lives of men like Jeremiah—or Albert Schweitzer. He granted men insight into his demands. This could be demonstrated in the lives of men like Isaiah—or Dag Hammarskjöld. The faith of Israel stressed not the ability of the mind to reflect upon God, but the ability of the mind *to act with God.* The emphasis was on the practical act of living in concert with Yahweh. One's ethics was closely connected with one's personal relation to God; and moral codes could provide no substitute for this relationship, though Israel often tried this, even as contemporary man tries to substitute law for justice, codes for relationships, paper for heart. This, then, was part of what was meant by a proper relation with God, and this was called in Israel the covenant. It was the most precious part of Israel's faith.

Covenant faithfulness can be identified in one's relations with other human beings. Anything that smacks of injustice, racism, and oppression of or indifference to one's fellow man indicates distance from God. All that demonstrates compassion and freedom and human dignity—and righteous wrath when it is necessary—indicates intimacy with God. The covenant faith, then, is always asking, "What does God require of me in this particular situation?" In every situation of life, whenever she was confronted by the need for a decision, Israel always asked, "Is it right or wrong?" She may not have known until she reflected upon it later in her history whether it *was* right or wrong, but she was required to make a decision.

The second ingredient in the covenant relation is this: God's will can be depended upon. For Israel the Exodus was a clear indication of what God intended, just as for Christians Jesus Christ should be a clear indication—or declaration—of what God intends. It was because of the Exodus that Israel chose to trust Yahweh. The great affirmation of the covenant was: "You shall be my people, and I shall be your God." In the phrase "You shall be my people," God declared his intent; and in the phrase "I shall be your God," Israel knew what it could depend upon.

The faith of Israel excluded all divine caprice and arbitrariness. The core of the problem of mankind's other religions (including much of what erroneously passes as Christianity) is the fear of "what God will do next." This seems to me to be the best reason for being an atheist. If we cannot depend on him, then there is no sense wasting time on him. Life is quite full enough of undependable things. To add one more and call it "god," is to take on just so much unnecessary baggage. I do not have time for an undependable God. But the faith of Israel says men know exactly where they stand in covenant relation to God.

There is an important and subtle distinction we must make here. God's dependability can never be defined by men. God alone defines his dependability, and he simply will not bind himself to men's definitions of it. What men must do is to read the terms of God's dependability on the basis of what he has done in the past and then to act upon that reading, to extrapolate from it.

It is in this way that Yahweh creates an atmosphere of trust and security. But the trust and security of God are not to be equated with vested interests, the status quo, law and order, the system, or the establishment. God's atmosphere of trust and stability may be equated with these kinds of things: that in any establishment engaged in blatant injustices, God will bring to ruin all such vested interests; that in any system which allows oppression, God will blot out and destroy that kind of status quo; that in any power structure which breeds inhumanity, God will uproot and cut off such laws and such order. The prophets of the Old Testament made this quite clear. God will not tolerate dehumanizing forces. And the prophets say, You can depend on that, You can trust it, You can live your life by it and feel secure.

This sense of security stimulates men to surrender their

wills to God's will, to become absorbed in his larger destiny, to give up their vested interests and territorial instincts, and to live for the larger good of the whole community. It turns men away from the past and toward the future in confidence and joy, assured that history is not a rudderless ship running headlong before a hurricane gale, but the arena in which slowly and painfully God's love is being evolved by mankind.

The covenant faith says we know what God is like. We are saddened and we mourn for the setbacks we see in the world around us, but we refuse to despair. God may bring down a nation or the nations, but only in order to build up. That is the true faith, the very core of it, and in this God we may trust. From this sense of dependence moral law can be determined and with it social order can be maintained. But these must not be derived from man's desires to preserve what he has and what he is. These may only be derived from God's desire for justice and humanness. Only on that basis may we have law and order.

For Christians all of this becomes personalized in Jesus the Christ. He is our given fact within history, as the Exodus was Israel's. He cannot be discovered through philosophy or doctrine or lessons. He can only be absorbed as a demonstration of faith in the covenant God. In this way, when we absorb him he breaks in upon us, molding our wills to his will, demanding our decision in every situation for his ethic, and turning us toward a future in which love is being evolved. It is through Jesus the Christ that we too are called into covenant relation with Almighty God.

## 2. The Uniqueness of Covenant Life

*Genesis 17:1-8*

This is certainly a time when the basic institutional structures with which we have been long familiar no longer command our allegiance or obedience. The state has lost its undisputed sovereignty over the loyalty of citizens. The political structure has broken down to such an extent that vast numbers of people are becoming apolitical. The family has been profoundly disrupted, so that it no longer exercises moral discipline as a social institution. Schools and universities are deeply uncertain about the nature of truth and how to communicate it. And the church faces an acute crisis, not only of how to articulate the faith but also of how to forge a community. A contemporary observer outside the church might describe it as "sloshing around," unable to commit itself radically to the basic ideals for which it says it stands.

Why is this so? I would suggest that it is because the Christian enterprise has lost its sense of covenant. In the preceding sermon we began to break open the meaning of the covenant faith. We looked at two insights that characterized Israel's self-understanding. First, God demonstrates himself in history, calling men to his will; and second, men who discern the will of God in history may depend upon his faithfulness.

From these two basic insights Israel extrapolated a further one: that persons who discern the will of God in history and act upon it in trust discover themselves in a unique position. This realization of a unique relationship between themselves and Yahweh their God is the key to Israel's self-understanding and her high ethic. Israel understood herself as a minority group with a very special uniqueness, and she acted very militantly as a minority. For Israel, everything depended on the special character that had been impressed on her by her relationship to Yahweh. As a minority community she awakened to the meaning of history as it unfolded all around her, and she began to discern the relentless evolution of the ethic of Love. This caused her to look forward to the future in hope.

At the same time individual Israelites awakened to the goals of their personal lives. They became conscious of how they participated in the unfolding ethic of Love, and this allowed them to face adversity with joy. But most important, this sense of uniqueness and of covenant awakened in Israel a sense of solidarity with all other human beings who discern and trust the will of God. Out of this sense of solidarity Israel was born. She was a remarkably unique community that not only realized her special covenant relationship with Yahweh her God, but also recognized her special covenant relationship with all other human beings. This is why Israel developed such a lofty ethical perspective.

Israel's unique covenant was forged on three things. First was her discernment of Yahweh's will. She looked at the Exodus and she knew his intention. Second was her utter dependence upon Yahweh her God. She looked back upon the wilderness experience and discovered that he had provided and that she would trust him. And third was her understanding of her own mission as his unique people. She was Yahweh's minority, bringing his love to the world. It was because of these three understandings that Israel never excluded the stranger or the sojourner or the oppressed or the disenfranchised. Uniqueness for Israel was not a sign of privilege but a sign of responsibility. Her task, her basic mission, was to absorb the stranger into the community of love. Thus Israel never existed for herself, but she always existed for others. Her unique covenant with Yahweh gave her a special mission to the world of men, and from this she derived hope and joy and her special sense of destiny.

If the contemporary Christian enterprise is uptight about anything, it is about this kind of uniqueness. Christians individually and the church corporately simply do not want to think in these terms. They want to think that the church represents a majority in the social order, which in fact it certainly does not. In consequence, Christians tend to respond to the church as to just another civic organization, like the Lions or the Rotary or Kiwanis. Many Christians want to make the church a faceless part of a faceless culture, because in a culture that is tending toward standardization anything that has a unique profile becomes uncomfortable. The result of this attitude is the complete breakdown of the covenant relationship with God, the inability to discern God's will in history, an uneasiness to trust its destiny to God, an unresponsiveness toward the unique mission of the church, and in many places in Christendom a resentful sense of abandonment, of hopelessness, of joylessness.

Given the situation in much of Christendom, the question can be asked, "Has the Christian enterprise, then, come to an end?" Some will argue cogently that indeed it has, and they can marshal a staggering amount of evidence to support their case. But some of us who are equally able to assess all of this about which we have just spoken can discern a different perspective. We are aware of a small enclave of Christians rediscovering the meaning of the covenant relationship and all the joy that goes with that— yes, the pain, the struggle too—but all the joy. We are aware of a small enclave of Christians who have a growingly incisive insight into God's self-demonstration in history, and this is giving these Christians an assurance of their own uniqueness. They are coming to understand Christianity as certainly a minority within the culture; but, even more crucial, they are coming to understand Christianity *as a minority in the church.* They are increasingly willing to act from a minority position with all that that entails. There is a growing responsiveness among them to the mission not of what has been called "Churchianity" but of covenant faith with God Almighty. This minority sees joy and hope, and it is important to recognize that it is becoming quite serious about its covenant consciousness.

This minority has a goal: to recapture Christ's church for Christ. Slowly but surely it will exert itself until it becomes the leaven within the church and social order that Jesus the Christ intended that it be. There is a solidarity among Christians with this insight, a solidarity that cannot be shaken. It is to these Christians who are renewing the covenant faith—rapidly in their own hearts, more slowly in the church and social orders—that the future belongs.

But the question can be raised: "Does not this attitude make this enclave exclusivist?" And the answer to that is: Never! This enclave is open to any human being who will, in seriousness, take up the covenant faith—not "philosophical religion" but the covenant faith. Is Jesus exclusive? Never! But he is unique. Under heaven he is unique; and in the same way this enclave is unique. And the enclave is totally unwilling to back away from this position. It will win. It will have the day, because the covenant community will be God's mission of Love.

So the larger question is: Who is willing to take up the covenant? Who is willing to become so faithful as to be forged into this kind of unique community? Is not that the question that is being asked of the whole church and of every individual Christian? Is not that the crucial question which will determine whether or not we face the future with fear or with steady nerve?

## 3. The Nerve of Covenant Life

*Exodus 24:1-11*

I have an idea that one of the most serious dilemmas facing us in the world today is loss of nerve. I see this in various manifestations. The political process seems to be completely unable to provide alternatives—the politicians have lost their nerve. We hear a lot of slogans and rhetoric about the social problems that face us, but few who mouth these have the nerve to face squarely the issues of human dignity involved. The church is unable to come to terms with its own uniqueness, seeking instead to remain a faceless part of a faceless culture. I have an uneasy intuition that people are retreating into themselves, losing their nerve.

So the question is: How do we gain nerve for living in these days? I suggest that the way is through a renewal of the covenant faith. By that I do not mean the insipid, wishy-washy Christian moralism that has been palmed off on us for so many generations now. I personally believe that this has done staggering damage to the covenant faith—so much damage, in fact, that even Christians have lost their nerve. But what kind of confidence, what kind of nerve, does the covenant faith inspire? I would suggest two things.

First, the covenant faith gives the believer nerve to face life with confidence in the goal of history. How often history seems to be nothing more than relentless fate, grinding on without any compassion for human need. But Israel had the nerve to declare that God was to be discovered *in this very history*; that faith grew out of the way history was experienced; and that faith was constantly being rekindled by the experience of history, so that God is discovered in the formation of people's social life. History becomes the field on which faith is practiced. The consequence of this is that contemporary history, the history of every generation, acquires a significant value of its own and every event demands an ethical decision.

Recently I attended a meeting of some local church leaders. We had to make a decision that would require us to take action on the allocation of $200,000 of the church's funds. I raised a question about our basic understanding of the church's mission as we were preparing to dispense the money—an uncomfortable question, because it demanded ethical commitments that few were prepared to make. I was told by the chairman of the group: "Now, David, this is just a procedural question, it is not a moral issue." The thing that really staggered me in that meeting was not so much the conflict I was having with the chairman and some of the other people there, as the fact that virtually nobody listened because for them it was not a moral decision! For many of the people who represent the Christian leadership of the church, a decision about allocating $200,000 was nothing more than a procedural question. Israel could never have understood that kind of thinking. She always understood history as going toward a goal, so that every decision was an ethical decision.

The goal to which Israel saw history moving was the Kingdom of God. The phrase, "the Kingdom of God," sounds unfamiliar to us today. Perhaps we might make it clearer by putting it in terms like this: the Christian understands the goal of history to be the realization of love throughout mankind. This is what the mission of the church is about: the actualization of love in humanity. This goal requires confidence in the value of love for human need, confidence in God's intention to see love prevail, confidence that all this can happen in the course of the historical process. And this confidence must be based on a sense of covenant with God. Only to those who are willing to renew the covenant in this generation will the gift of confidence be forthcoming. Israel understood that it was up to every generation to renew the covenant. Our task is to renew it in our own time and to become an enclave with nerve in a society that has lost its nerve.

There is a second kind of confidence that the covenant faith gives the believer: the nerve to face life with confidence in the universal destiny of mankind. Not only is there a goal to history, there is a destiny toward which man is evolving. We hear a lot these days about "the universal man in the global village," but these are stock phrases that do not really mean much. Nationalism and imperialism have never appeared more vicious than they do in the world today. Yet the Christian man must always recognize himself as a universal man. In the ancient religions each nation chose its god. There was an indissoluble link between god and country. The deity was nothing more than an external part of the national self-consciousness. Apart from the people a god did not exist or, if he existed, he was isolated and impotent. Thus in ancient religions—and this is very important—the nations elected their gods, and the god's job was to behave. Thus there was no sense of ethical obligation on the part of the nation or the person.

Israel brought a whole new perspective. It is difficult for us to grasp just how crucial this is. We are on the threshold here of a major development in the history of human thought. Israel did not elect Yahweh. Yahweh elected Israel. Israel did not form the covenant. Yahweh formed it out of his grace. Yahweh was not dependent on Israel. Israel was dependent on Yahweh. Yahweh owned Israel. Israel never owned Yahweh. Do you see what fantastic importance this has in the understanding of the evolution of love? For the first time in history it was not a god's behavior that was at stake, but the people's behavior. Do you see the difference that Israel brought? Herein lies the very foundation of human ethics. It makes a difference, according to Israel, how men treat each other. People sometimes ask why I place so much emphasis on the covenant. It is because of issues like this. We cannot understand our faith until we understand the meaning of this covenant, and we cannot act responsibly until we understand our faith.

Now the most important extrapolation of this insight is this: *the will of God can never be identified with national interests.* American Christianity has had enormous trouble on this point. There is a strong tendency for Americans to identify patriotism with faithfulness, to confuse manifest destiny with God's destiny, to identify our national interests with religious insight. We have been a people dedicated to freedom and justice and dignity. That is our heritage as a nation—a noble heritage of which we should be deeply proud. And, after all, these are some of God's main interests too. But because these interests are also God's interests, we have come to the point where we cannot differentiate between God and the nation. The result is that we have a feeling—or have had for a long time—that God blesses everything we do. Religion in America has become an extension of our national self-consciousness.

But the identification of God's will with America's national interests is no longer convincing for anyone who reads his daily newspaper. Freedom is bleeding to death in Vietnam; justice is being brought down to utter disaster in our city streets; human dignity screams at us with a twisted and tortured face from our ghettos. We can no longer believe that God blesses us; and more terrible still, we cannot even pretend that we do any more. This is a new trauma for American culture and we are not handling it very well. We have never felt such guilt before as a people, and we are angry, and we thrash about for anybody to dump that anger on.

The only way that we will survive with honest hope is with the Christian perspective of the universal destiny of mankind. Teilhard de Chardin says, "The age of the nations is past and now it is time to start building the earth." One might look at contemporary neo-nationalism and argue that there is not much to be said for this contention. But I believe that this is nothing more than the last gasps of a gradually dying nationalism. The nations are dying, they are giving up their ghosts—and that includes the United States. This process may take us several hundred years, but that is a short time in human history. Out of this death-process a new universal order is being forged, and that is what Christianity is after anyway!

The future belongs not to those who mourn the death of gods of the nations, but to those who greet God, the God of the covenant, as he unfolds his destiny for all mankind. Jesus grasped God's design of love as taught by Israel's covenant faith and projected this vision into what all men could be. He lived a unique life that demonstrated the uniqueness of all men. His living was an actualization of what the human social order is to be like. He called it the "Kingdom of God," which, we have suggested, may be translated as "the universal dominance of love." The point is that Jesus had the nerve to live that kind of life because of his covenant with God.

The world today is crying for a vision. The Christian is in a unique position to provide a vision of confidence in the goal of history and in the destiny of mankind. This is going to take a great deal of steady nerve, and it is only going to come on the part of those Christians—the enclave in the church—who are willing and ready to renew the covenant faith. The world today is crying for nerve; and, as never before, Christians can provide that nerve. This will depend on those who are prepared to enter into a unique covenant with God and their brothers, because only such people will fully understand the unique intentions God has for human life, and only such people can fully demonstrate in their own lives the unique love that will spur mankind forward. The world needs nerve. Covenant Christians can have it; and, most important, they can *give* it.

## 4. The Risk of Covenant Life

*II Samuel 7:8-16*

William Faulkner, when asked to define Christianity, said this: "Christianity is every individual's individual code of individual behavior by means of which he makes himself a better human being than his nature wants to be." My guess is that there are significant numbers of Christians who would subscribe to that viewpoint. To look at Christianity this way is to try to fit God into our expectations so that we may avoid having to fit ourselves to God's expectations. It is an attempt to package God in a box of human presuppositions. It represents an enormous perversion of the Christian faith. Jesus stands against everything that that statement stands for.

The people of Israel made an equally critical miscalculation. Under their covenant through Moses, Israel really did try to fit itself to Yahweh's expectations. They were willing to risk a covenant relation with their God Yahweh. But under the new covenant with David, a new understanding began to emerge. God was seen as having obligations. God would never forsake Israel under any conditions. He might punish her, but he would never abandon her. This was an attempt to package God, to limit him to a nation, Israel; to limit him to a place, Zion; to limit him to an attitude of promise that he has made and now cannot break. It was an attempt to confine God's freedom, to box him in, to nail him down, to package him. It was a desire to take the risk out of covenant life, and it represented an

29

enormous perversion of the faith of Israel. Yet this perversion became the faith by which Israel lived for centuries.

From perversions of faith such as the two we have just described we gain this important insight into our covenant relation with God: that God enters freely the relationship a man has with him, and God may end it at any time. Thus the covenant relation with God involves an enormous risk. Any attempt to coerce God is utterly futile. God exists beyond the person or the nation or the church. His reality cannot be confined. The risk that man takes is that God may choose to abandon the faithless. This shocks many Christians, who think that they have God in their pocket. They ask, "Is this a loving God?" I suggest that it is time we quit being sloppy about the meaning of love. If men refuse to be loving, then the most loving thing God can do is to judge them. God does not create more love in the world by being sentimental toward unloving people. I suspect there are many unloving people who are trying to sneak by on God's sentimentality. That will not work. God has lots of love but he has no sentiment.

God voluntarily initiates the covenant relationship with man. God voluntarily sends Jesus to be the Christ. These things are done out of his free grace. In human covenants both partners have obligation. In God's covenant only man has obligations—to do justice, to love mercy, to walk humbly with God. God has no obligation because what he does is a free gift. God may judge, punish, and abandon faithless and unloving people.

It makes many Christians angry when we talk in terms like this, because it means that the covenant is no longer a safe bulwark behind which we can hide. It means that it can no longer be used to bolster our personal righteousness or to prop up the status quo of the churches. We suddenly realize that the covenant relationship involves danger and risk. If you have read the previous sermons you may ask, "But earlier you said that the covenant God is a dependable God. Now what kind of dependability is this?" I think that is a fair question, and we can ask what is the measure of God's dependability. For what can we depend upon God?

Christians can depend on God to destroy the oppressor, and lift up the oppressed. Christians can depend on God to bring down the unjust, and exalt the disenfranchised. Christians can depend on God to overthrow the wealthy, and succor the poor. These are great things upon which to depend. But there is more. Christians can also depend on God not to bless any national interests that are inhuman, not to preserve a status quo that is unjust, not to shore up a power structure that is oppressive, not to protect any establishment that is self-righteous. When nations act as the Soviet Union acted in Czechoslovakia or as the United States has acted in Vietnam, judgment will be brought against them and their actions. The USSR has lost all hope of credibility in the community of nations: no one will believe her any more. The United States has lost her international integrity and her dignity at home. Judgment is being rendered; we can depend on that.

In American culture there is enough wealth so that every single family in this nation may enjoy the benefits of their own three-bedroom home, of enough food and enough clothing, of a college education for every single child who is capable of achieving one. We have enough wealth to do all this, and yet poverty and malnutrition and ignorance and slums are rampant. God will provoke rebellion in the poor that will tear a culture like that apart. It is happening. The judgment is being rendered; we can depend upon it. Around the world governments, including parts of the United States government, are trying to suppress the voice of young people who are crying out against the injustices of the industrial revolution. God will strengthen the voice of youth until injustices blessed by the old power structure come crashing down upon the heads of the unheeding and the unlistening. All over the world it is happening. The judgment is being rendered—we can depend upon it.

Jesus understood all this and tried to interpret it. For

his trouble he was crucified. The world still crucifies the young and the poor and the disenfranchised and the peacemakers and those who would speak truth. Jesus was willing to risk crucifixion to do what God wanted done. The same risk is being asked today of those who want a relationship with God. The person who is in covenant with God has to risk doing what God wants done. Man does not define what is to be done; God defines it.

God wants us to feed the hungry. Who among us is willing to forgo one meal a day for a week and take the money that we save and send it to UNICEF or Church World Service to aid the starving?

God wants us to clothe the naked. Many Christians have given generously of their old clothes to various social services, but I wager that none of us has given so generously that he cannot go back to his closet and find more clothes to be given away. We *can* spare it; will we?

God wants us to house the homeless. Many of us have loans for many different things. Who is willing to borrow more money to be shared with a family in the ghetto so that they too may have decent housing?

This is the stance that Jesus took. He did these kinds of things as God's Anointed. He also got killed for it. The covenant relationship is a risky business. Who here dares to take those kinds of risks? To the one who is willing God freely extends his covenant. This is his gracious love. He blesses the man who is willing to take that risk. From the man who is unwilling God freely withdraws his covenant. This is his gracious love. He judges that man—but the judgment and the wrath are also the measure of God's love.

We had better get that straight. Too often Christians are way off base on that point. To belong to the covenant community means to be ready to risk God's love. God is utterly dependable; we can depend on him. He will exalt the man who will take the risk, and bring down gracious love. The covenant faith lays on a man the love of God, a love that may lift him up in joy and hope or bring him down in wrath and judgment. It is a risk. Are we ready to take that kind of risk? It demands involvement without reservation. It lays claim upon the whole person and upon the whole church. Are we as persons and as a church ready to risk that kind of covenant?

## 5. The Mark of Covenant Life

*Jeremiah 31:27-34*

Every group of people who seek to live in relationship to each other must have identifying marks by which that relationship becomes evident. We see this within our society—dinner parties and cocktail parties are outward manifestations of relationships between people. In such cases the relationships tend to be very superficial. In the Christian community public worship becomes the identifying mark by which we know who is in the faithful community. Those people who are "in the covenant" worship together. The people who do not worship together are not "in the covenant" regardless of what they may call themselves.

Israel, as she understood herself as a covenant community, also needed, and had, identifying marks. There were two of these. First, she needed a place where the covenant was inscribed. She had this in the tables of the law, stone tables on which the Mosaic covenant was written. Second, she needed a sign to indicate that the covenant had been accepted. This was circumcision, the sign in Israel of response to the covenant. Soon these two signs or marks became misinterpreted as guarantees, and the covenant of Moses was replaced with the covenant of David. Risk was replaced with security, responsibility with privilege. Israel saw herself as irresistible to Yahweh.

Given these circumstances, Yahweh had no alternative but to love her. And so he did. He loved Israel. The direction his love took was to bring her down to destruction for her injustice, her oppression, and her self-

34

righteousness. As a sign of his love, in 721 B.C. he destroyed the Northern Kingdom. As a sign of his love, in 586 B.C. he destroyed the Southern Kingdom. Israel was brought to her knees. (What parent who disciplines a child does not know the very subtle ramifications of this kind of love?) But this was interpreted by Israel as a manifestation of Yahweh's great concern for his children.

I would suggest to you that Christians fail to take these facts very seriously. We say, "Why, God would never do such things as that to us." In effect, we are saying God owes us fealty, that we are the Lord and he is our serf. So we revert to the whole idea of the covenant with David. We abstract and intellectualize God until we consider him powerless. But Israel knew God's love in terms of wrath and judgment. Because we refuse to accept this lesson, I would suggest, the church is in the shape it is in today.

Jeremiah lived during the period between the fall of the Northern Kingdom and the fall of the Southern Kingdom. What Jeremiah desperately tried to do was interpret these dimensions of God's love. He had a good grasp of what God's love involved. It involved promise but also doom. It involved renewal but also judgment. As we read in our passage of Scripture, God comes to build and to plant only after he has plucked up and broken down. What Jeremiah was interested in was clearing away all the miscalculation about God's love. Jeremiah was given the high privilege of announcing God's new covenant with his people. Just as the old covenant had two identifying marks, so did the new. First, the new covenant would be inscribed. But it would be inscribed upon the inner life of the individual and the community, not upon stone tablets. And secondly, it would be sealed, not in a physical act, but on the hearts of faithful men—what St. Paul calls the "circumcision of the heart." Jeremiah's intent was to destroy the notions of security and privilege that Israel had associated with the covenant with David and to restore the idea of risk and responsibility on which the covenant with Moses was based.

There are several important ingredients to this new covenant. First, the new covenant of the heart is a free gift of God. God initiates it. Man does not create the covenant; man only responds to the grace of God. Second, the new covenant of the heart rests on God's forgiveness. God in the wrath of his love brings men to their knees. He disciplines their unlovingness and their unlovableness. He shatters their pride and destroys their self-sufficiency. But he breaks down in order that he may build up. And when men respond and return to God, then God rejoices with open arms and with total acceptance. This is the meaning of Jesus' Parable of the Prodigal Son. Most Christians totally misunderstand this parable. Jesus is not talking about a young man who goes out and commits a few sins and comes back to receive his father's forgiveness. Jesus is talking about the relationship of the covenant community to its God. This is what the covenant community has done and this is the response of its Father.

A third ingredient of this new covenant of the heart is that it exists at the very center of man's being. Men are called to make a personal response to the personal invitation of God. God fills the vacuum that exists at the center of our existence. How many of us do not know at times that terrible vacuum! I would suggest that for most contemporary Christians God is very remote. He is not at the center of life. If God does come into life at all, he comes in on the very edge. If we were honest, the prayer that we begin, "Oh God, who is deep within me," would probably begin, "Oh God, who is on the farthest periphery of my life." For increasing numbers of people, to introduce God is to introduce what is most remote in their personal experience. Even among Christians God is not understood at the heart of things. The new covenant rights this relationship. It puts God back at the center, back at the heart of things.

Finally, the new covenant of the heart creates a new community. The old Israel was judged and forsaken because of her loss of heart. In his love for her, God brought her to destruction, for he will not tolerate anti-love to prevail. But then he creates the possibility of a whole new response. A new people are called into existence—a new race of men, that is how Paul defines it. We are not just men in the world like other men. Christians are different men; they are a new race—a new race born of the relationships of love.

This is what Jeremiah came and offered as the new covenant of the heart. Because of God's promise through Jeremiah, Israel—as persons and as a community—now had the choice of beginning again. Israel could have a new heart that would bring new relations between mankind and God, between brothers in the faith, and, yes, even between the nations. What happened instead was that Israel had a massive heart attack. Jeremiah told her what her sickness was, but she ignored the diagnosis. She went on insisting on her exclusive position, her privilege, her security. She insisted on maintaining the status quo. She continued in her unloving ways of injustice and oppression and exploitation of the poor, and the result of this was that she had massive heart failure. Yahweh brought her to destruction, and she was kept in the coronary care unit for several centuries. She remained in this moribund state until she was restored to life by a man named Jesus who was called the Christ.

In Jesus God once again took the initiative. Jesus demonstrates what being human really means. In Jesus God once again extends his forgiving love. He breaks us down for our failure to be fully human beings, and he reveals his burning wrath of judgment. But he lifts us up to become what we may be so that we may exult in the glorious refreshment of his blessing. In Jesus God speaks once again to the very center of our being. He dwells again in the center of our life. He gives us the option of no longer being remote and distant. In Jesus God creates a new community, a new race of men based upon risk and responsibility, a community that will sustain and support each other, a community that will go to war against everything that is unloving in the world, a community that will demonstrate to the world the dimensions of God's love. Jesus, who was called the Christ, put the heart back into God's enterprise among men. Through skillful maneuvers ranging from fibrillation to transplant, he got that heart going again. Jesus did what Jeremiah could not do. He saved the patient.

Now there is much speculation that the patient is on the verge of another heart failure. And there is much evidence to indicate that this time it will be much more serious than the last. In fact, the illness may be terminal. There are many who think that the church as God's enterprise is dying. This seems to me to sell God extraordinarily short. I can see the evidence for their argument, but beyond that I can see this as a time when God in his love—his marvelous, gracious love—is bringing his children to judgment. We as Christians have failed him. The church, as a corporate covenant community throughout the world, has failed him. And he will bring us to love for that failure.

But remember, when God breaks us down he will build us up. And I would suggest to you that the Christian enterprise is on the verge of its most creative era. The clue is found in the thought of Teilhard de Chardin, who says that God dwells incognito in the heart of all things. What Jesus has done is to give the Christian the unique insight that God exists in the heart of all things. If we are in covenant with God, this above everything should be our experience of covenant: that we know God in the heart of things. That is the responsibility of the Christian, both as person and as community, to identify God in the heart of things. The world needs this identification terribly. This is what Jeremiah tried to do, and he failed. This is what Jesus tried to do, and he succeeded. And in his success Christians can now bring insight to help the world see when God blesses and when God curses; and to see how both blessing and cursing are manifestations of God's gracious and tender love toward his people.

Christians have the unique opportunity to assimilate and

absorb this insight into their personal lives and into their corporate lives as the church. We can be living demonstrations of God's love. There is a risk in this, because we may fail as Jeremiah failed. But there is also hope, because we may succeed as Jesus succeeded. Be it success or failure, that is the mark of covenant life.

## 6. The Renewal of Covenant Life

We live in a day when much of life is superficial. We yearn for the inward experiences that count for something—those experiences which delight our souls the most, which inspire us to the most noble sensitivities, when we know that deep communion, that profound fellowship with God, those rare moments when we are once again sure that there is a link. The Israelites had a word for that link and that word was "covenant." It was the covenant that formed the link between God and man and between man and man.

As the Israelites understood their covenant they felt two needs: to identify other people who also understood and felt and knew that same covenant and to renew their covenant. To meet these two needs, Israel went up once a year to the high place at Shechem. There at the holy shrine she renewed her covenant with the Lord. All the tribes that identified Yahweh as their God came together. The priests read the law, the cultic prophets commented upon it, and then in a grand covenant ceremony they repeated what Moses had done. They sacrificed a lamb, took the blood, threw it against the altar, and then on the people; and they said, "Yes, once again the covenant is sealed. For this generation the covenant is new."

Israel's profound insight was that you cannot seal the covenant once and for all and be done with it. The covenant must be renewed in every generation. Each new generation had to accept God again and discover the link between itself and its God.

Jesus understood this too, and he said to those who would follow him, "We must keep this covenant because it is a very fragile and very holy thing." So he gave us ways and means to identify who the people of the covenant are today and to renew that covenant once again in our own lives and as a community of faithful people. That is why we come to the table of Holy Communion: so that we may identify each other and say, "Yes, here are my brothers in the covenant. Here are those people who do not want to live just on the surface but seek this deeper, this profound, this inner understanding. I covenant with God and with them. I know who they are." But also, we come to the table so that we too may renew that covenant. Not only is it necessary to renew it in each generation; but everyone who really understands it, understands something more: that it is necessary to renew it again and again. We will fall from the grace of covenant life, and we have to come back and renew it again. But the gift God gives us is to come back to his table and repeat the solemn rituals of ancient Israel. We identify each other and gain strength because we are all his covenant people. We renew that covenant which we have with each other and with God so that once again we may walk in his way.

## 7. The Joy of Covenant Life

*I Samuel 25:29*

We have been reflecting in the preceding six sermons on the meaning of covenant life. Now we come to the end of that series. We have been trying to discover what it means to belong to the covenant Christian community. The concluding thought that I would like to share with you is this: to belong to the covenant community means to participate in a life of *joy*. This is the highest, most supreme, noblest, paramount point of covenant living: that we participate together shoulder to shoulder in a life of joy.

For many people life is nothing more than a series of encounters. It is not a continuum of relationships. Encounter may provide tension that can at times be very creative, but it will seldom provide joy. There must be encounters in Christian life, but it is more important in the covenant community of Christians that there be a continuum of relationships. The covenant life says that joy is only to be found in relationships with other human beings and with God. In other words, joy is found as we are, in the words of the text, "bound in the bundle of the living in the care of the Lord." That is the secret of Christianity. That is the secret of covenant life.

Christians, it is the only secret of ultimate and profound joy. When your brother struggles, you too share his torment; and when he conquers, you share his victory. In the hour of his sin, you share with him his guilt; and when he repents, you share his forgiveness. In the moment of his despair, you share his darkness; and when he has pleasure, you know his gaiety. In the hour of his hate (and Christians do hate), you share his frustration; and in the hour of his love, you share his joyful thanks. In the hour of your brother's sadness, you have learned how to weep with him; and when he laughs, his laughter gladdens your heart. When he walks through the shadow of death, then you walk beside him in the valley; and when he comes up to a life of renewal, then you too share that rebirth. In the time of his moral weakness, you too are timid with him; but when he stands righteous and tall, you share his high resolve. When he is conceited, in him you know your own false pride; but when he finally looks at himself honestly, you too gain insight into your life. In the time of his temptation, you feel the loss of strength and the weakness in your own soul; but when he stands firm, you share his integrity. In the time of his deepest pain, you share his terrible affliction; but when he sees the light of hope, you too see that vision. In his time of doubt (and Christians do doubt), you too know the terrible uncertainty of his soul; but when he discovers faith, then you rejoice because you share his Christ.

That is the meaning of covenant life. It is the only way for us to know joy in the world. This is the measure of God's beauty: that we are bound in the bundle of the living in the care of the Lord.

# A Litany for Covenant Life

*Liturgist:* We are bound in the bundle of the living in the care of the Lord.

*People:* Christian, in the hour of your struggle, I too share your torment; when you conquer, grant me to share your victories.

*Liturgist:* We are bound in the bundle of the living in the care of the Lord.

*People:* Christian, in the hour of your sin, I too share your guilt; when you repent, grant me to share your forgiveness.

*Liturgist:* We are bound in the bundle of the living in the care of the Lord.

*People:* Christian, in the hour of your despair, I too share your darkness; when you see the light of hope, grant me to share your vision.

*Liturgist:* We are bound in the bundle of the living in the care of the Lord.

*People:* Christian, in the hour of your pain, I too share your affliction; when you have pleasure, grant me to share your gaiety.

*Liturgist:* We are bound in the bundle of the living in the care of the Lord.

*People:* Christian, in the hour of your hate, I too share your frustration; when you are full of love, grant me to share your thankful joy.

*Liturgist:* We are bound in the bundle of the living in the care of the Lord.

*People:* Christian, in the hour of your sadness, I too weep with you; when you laugh, grant me to share your gladness.

*Liturgist:* We are bound in the bundle of the living in the care of the Lord.

*People:* Christian, in the shadow of death, I walk in the valley beside you; when the spirit of renewal overtakes you, grant me to share that birth.

*Liturgist:* We are bound in the bundle of the living in the care of the Lord.

*People:* Christian, in your time of moral weakness, I am timid with you; when righteousness leads you on, grant me to share that high resolve.

*Liturgist:* We are bound in the bundle of the living in the care of the Lord.

*People:* Christian, in your self-conceit, I too know my own false pride; when you discover yourself honestly, grant me to share that insight.

*Liturgist:* We are bound in the bundle of the living in the care of the Lord.

*People:* Christian, in the time of your temptation, I too lose my strength; when you stand firm, grant me to share your integrity.

*Liturgist:* We are bound in the bundle of the living in the care of the Lord.

*People:* Christian, in your time of doubt, I too share your uncertainty; when you discover faith, grant me to share your Christ.

*All:* We are bound in the bundle of the living in the care of the Lord.

PART TWO

# THE COVENANT COMMUNITY
# IS THREATENED AND RESPONDS

## 8. The Danger of Covenant Life

### Amos 5:21-24

The whole purpose of the covenant community is to create a climate in which love can evolve. The response of the world is at worst to destroy such a climate, at best to neutralize it. Destruction is easier to deal with because we can identify it. We know it for what it is. Neutralization is much more insidious because it removes Christ's values in the name of Christianity, making discernment very hard for Christians and confusing and demoralizing us. It is at this point that Satan is playing his best game.

The issue here is the adjustment of the covenant community to the surrounding environment. For Israel this was a crucial confrontation. She had left Egypt and settled in the land of Canaan, with its highly developed culture and highly sophisticated religion. She was face to face with the god of Canaan, even as Christians today are confronted by the god of American nationalism. In that age, it was the Israelite's sense of history confronting the Canaanite's sense of nature; today it is Christianity confronting "Churchianity." For them it was the confrontation between an ethic in which righteousness and justice were the main ingredients and the Canaanite approach to life not much concerned with the needs of one's brother; for us the crisis is the choice between the Way of Jesus and the way of shrewd practicality. (We hear that even in church meetings: we must be "shrewd and practical.") What the Canaanite culture was trying to do was to absorb the Israelite faith, to assimilate it and thus distort it so that

49

it was unrecognizable. It was trying to turn faith into religion.

What is the difference between faith and religion? I would suggest this: faith stands *over against* the culture, providing a dimension of insight, a kind of conscience out of which emerges a highly ethical motivation, a concern for other human beings. Religion, on the other hand, stands *within* the culture, providing the culture blessing and support, and the "morality of religion" is the "desire of the people." I suggest that all this is part of the current crisis in the contemporary covenant community, the Christian church. We are living in a time when the culture is desperately trying to absorb the faith. We are confronted with an attempt on the part of the world to assimilate and absorb Christianity, to turn the covenant faith into a religion of the social order. The world is trying to neutralize Christianity. This is happening in at least two significant ways.

The first is the depersonalization of the God-man relation. This is an attempt on the part of the world to neutralize or destroy the covenant, because if this can be done then the possibilities of love can be eliminated. In Israel this took the form of questioning Yahweh's sovereignty. Some said, "Well, yes, Yahweh may be the God of history, but Yahweh is not the God of nature; therefore, we as men must depend upon the nature god, the Baal." Today it takes the form of questioning the sovereignty of love. There is real suspicion in our world that love cannot win out in the end, that people cannot learn to live together in harmony, that nations cannot discover the joy of justice and righteousness. There seems to be much evidence to support these suspicions. Thus, man must depend upon his own devices. He must control and manipulate his destiny. (It is out of this kind of thinking that we get the rationale for the "necessary war.")

What happens here is an attempt to harness God to human expectations. God's moral will is controlled according to man's immediate desires. Man assimilates God into himself. The question is often asked me (and I am sure you hear it too—if you do not ask it at times), "Is God anything but a creation of man's imagination?" I would suggest that if this is so, this God—if he is not already dead—ought to be killed. Men try to restrict God. They try to restrict him to land, to nationalize him. We do that in this country; God is a good American. Men try to restrict God to a particular people, to a certain kind of culture, for if they can localize and legalize him, they can domesticate him. In such a situation as this it becomes very fashionable to be religious. In such a situation as this it is in God's interest not to overdo his demands. He should tailor his requirements to meet men's desires. He should require only what men are willing to deliver. And if God goes beyond these limits, then men can merely opt out and have done with it. What this situation does is to neutralize the God-man relationship. The entire covenant bond is shattered—God is depersonalized. And in depersonalizing God, man depersonalizes himself.

This is exactly the crisis the covenant community faces today. The church is being told not to overdo its demands. It is being told to tailor its requirements to fit the members' desires. Should it overstep these limits, then the members will opt out. They will remove their support—in other words, their presence or their finances; and both of these are the criteria by which "success" is adjudged in the modern church.

Jesus faced this same set of circumstances in his life, and he chose the response of faithfulness. The result of his faithfulness was a momentary breaking down. Everything fell apart. He was crucified. But out of that momentary breaking down came a stupendous building up, on through his resurrection, to the church, in which the covenant relation was once again restored and the God-man relationship re-personalized. The same situation is occurring in contemporary churches. There is a shaking down of the Christian enterprise. Vast numbers of former Christians are opting out. The demands of the covenant life are just too great. God in his church has overstepped his limits. And it is thus becoming less and less "fashionable" to be a Christian in the world today. But on the other side there is a miraculous building up of the new covenant community. Countless Christians are for the first time in their lives discovering within themselves a really burning zeal. They are becoming eager to be caught up in God's design to realign the God-man relationship and to re-personalize the covenant. It is here that the future of covenant love lies. It is here that Jesus is still alive as God's Christ in the world. It is here that love is evolving, however painfully that may be.

The second way the world is trying to neutralize Christianity is by replacing faith with religion. The world wants to institutionalize and entrench all of the religious apparatus, because if it can do that it can so encumber the faith as to make it immobile, inoperative. Remember now—faith stands over against the culture, providing a dimension of conscience that results in a high ethic: good is what God requires of man. Religion stands within the culture providing support and blessing for that culture, resulting in an amoral kind of situation: good is what people desire. So the critical issue is between the covenant faith and institutionalized religion, between Christianity and "Churchianity," between personalized relations and ritualized action.

The covenant faith has great demands of personal ethical responsibility. It continually asks the question: Are we about what Jesus would be about? And it asks this of the person and of the community and of the nation and of the church. The religious apparatus, on the other hand, never addresses this question, because it is much too threatening. The religious apparatus is concerned with pretentious cultic practice, with the meritorious works of believers, with the perpetuation of the institution. The result of all of this is that the ethical response to the needs of human beings evaporates. Religion is manipulated to meet the needs of the religious person, not the needs of the world.

So man's relation to God is externalized and depersonalized.

This is the crisis in which many Christians find themselves today. Religion has rendered faith lifeless. Meaningless motions have replaced trustful self-surrender. Calculated morality has replaced ethical risk. Religion has become a con game in which we try to get God to do our bidding. And two things are happening. First, those people who view the church as a pliable, religious apparatus are becoming desperately disturbed. They need much loving concern from covenant Christians. They are confused and they need much light. They need someone to say to them, "Return and find joy, not in the machinations of religion, but in the fellowship of people working together." And second, those who view the church as a place where true covenant relations can happen are becoming fantastically excited. The church is shifting, Christians. The church is shifting from an entrenched religious institution to a faithful covenant community.

The attempts of the world to destroy and neutralize Christ's vision are thwarted; and a whole new climate is emerging, a climate in which faith is surfacing above religion, in which the God-man relation is being re-personalized, in which the covenant community is taking very seriously its reason for being. Now, in this climate, the Christian can once again look with hope and joy to a world in which love can evolve. And that, after all, is the only reason for being Christian.

## 9. The Covenant Community Announces Its Vocation

### Isaiah 61:1-9

Israel understood that the vocation of the covenant life was to create a climate in which love could evolve. The world set against her all manner of powers deliberately designed to destroy the possibility for covenant life and covenant love to evolve.

Israel responded to the world's attacks in two ways. First, the covenant community announced publicly its unique vocation. Israel had discovered her vocation in the Exodus. Yahweh had chosen her, had elected her, and had called her out to a specific task in specific terms. Amos announced these terms: "Let justice roll down like waters, and righteousness like an ever-flowing stream." Micah announced them: "What does the Lord require of you, O man, but to do justice and to love steadfast mercy and to walk humbly with your God." And Isaiah announced them: "To bring good news to the afflicted, to bind up the broken-hearted, to proclaim liberty to the captives, to set free those who are bound, to comfort everyone who mourns, to build up that which lies in ruin, to love justice and to hate wrong." Thus Israel's vocation was based not on being "religious," but on being faithful and obedient. Israel's vocation was based not on morality, not on keeping rules, but on the ethics of how you love another man. Israel's vocation was based not on rituals before Yahweh but on relationships with Yahweh.

Jesus brought this sense of vocation into sharp focus. John the Baptist asked Jesus, "Are you the one or shall we expect another?" And Jesus replied, "What do you see? The blind are given their sight, the deaf hear, the lame walk, the lepers are cleansed, the poor have hope." Jesus understood himself as chosen by God for a specific task; his vocation was to make real in the lives of men the insights of Amos and Micah and Isaiah. He summed it all up when he said, "When you do it to your brother, you do it to me."

This is the vocation of the contemporary church, the contemporary covenant community: to make real the insights of Amos, Micah, and Isaiah, to do it unto the very least of our brothers. The vocation of the covenant community is to be Christlike in a world filled with loneliness, fear, and suspicion, with hatred, war, and oppression, with hunger, pain, and disease. That is the business that the covenant community is called to be about.

This local church claims to be God's faithful people. Are we letting justice roll down like waters? From this fellowship are righteous relations being created among men? Is this covenant community in some way demonstrating steadfast mercy to its enemies? Are we carrying good news to afflicted people? Are we binding up the brokenhearted? Are we giving liberty to captives? Are we opening the prisons of those who are bound? Are we about the business of bringing comfort to those who mourn? Is this vocation of this church consciously, publicly declared and announced?

But let us not forget that the vocation of the covenant community is possible only when it is the vocation of each individual Christian. If you were asked what your vocation is, what would you answer—your job, your daily work? If you were asked what your priorities are, how would you list them—first, my family; second, my job; third, my community; fourth, my nation? Those are the responses the world wants you to give, but they are not the proper responses of a Christian. They are not the proper responses of a man who is in covenant relation with God. His vocation is to be God's obedient and faithful son, and his priority is to do what God's love requires him to do, wherever he is, whatever he is doing, whomever he is with.

When was the last time that justice rolled out of your life? When did you last create righteous relations among men? Name the last time you were merciful to someone who was hostile to you. How did you last give good news to some terribly afflicted soul? Where was the last place that you bound up a broken heart? When you found a man captive to his fears and his torments, did you set him free? When you found a man imprisoned by his prejudices and his hatreds and his hostilities, did you undo his chains? The whole world mourns. How are you bringing it comfort?

It is easy for one to talk about Israel, or about Jesus, or about "the church." But it is tough for one to talk about himself. Yet that is where it must begin. Only when we discover vocation within ourselves can we engage in vocation in the church, and only then can the church inform and sustain our inner vocation. Only when the covenant relation with God is very personal can we know the meaning of the covenant vocation in the community. And then the community can provide strength that will keep our personal covenant relation with God in order.

Besides responding to the world's attacks by publicly announcing its vocation, the covenant community announces that it has power to achieve this vocation. This whole business of vocation is not just a pleasant idea. This is God's gracious gift. It is the power of his Holy Spirit. Translated into modern terms, it is the *energy* of his love. Israel knew Yahweh's energy loose within her. The Exodus was her point of reference. Yahweh had actually released captives and bound up the brokenhearted and opened their prisons. He had lifted them up in their affliction. Yahweh's vocation was Israel's experience. And Israel took Yahweh's vocation to herself as her vocation. She accepted and appropriated his energy as her energy.

Jesus knew God's energy of love loose within him. Because of this energy of love the blind did see and the lame did walk and the deaf did hear and the poor did have good news. God's vocation was fulfilled in Jesus because Jesus accepted God's vocation and his energy. Thus Jesus, the Christ, became the first fully human being.

The contemporary church, the covenant community, has God's energy loose within it. Its point of reference is Jesus the Christ. This world is blind. Will the church release energy that will make it see? This world is deaf. Will the church release energy that will make it hear? This world is lame. Will the church (will this local church) release energy that will make it walk again? The world is poverty-stricken. Will the church release hope?

The question is not whether the covenant community has the energy—this is guaranteed by God. This is his gracious gift. The question is: Will we use it? If the covenant community will use this energy, she becomes, in Peter's words, a chosen race, a royal priesthood, a holy nation, God's own people, declaring the wonderful deeds of him who called her out of darkness into his marvelous light. This is the question the church must address—the question about the faithful use of God's energy of love.

But if the church must address it, so must every individual Christian. The person to the right of you, look at him, he is blind. Do you care enough to help him see? The person to the left of you, look at him, he is lame. Do you have love enough to help him walk? The person in front of you, look at him, he is deaf. Do you care enough to help him hear? The person behind you, can you feel his eyes upon you, he has a leprosy of guilt. Can you extend a hand that will help him to be healed? We are all poverty-stricken, every one of us. Dare we engage in a covenant so deep that we can help each other hope?

Our point of reference in all of this is the covenant community. It—the covenant community—is called by God to be Christ to the world. But *we are it*—thus we are called to be Christ to each other and to the world. This is our vocation. With it we can take on the world, because whatever we do to our brothers, we do to Christ.

## 10. The Universality of Uniqueness

*Isaiah 19:18-24*

In a previous sermon we thought together about how the covenant life demands great risks on the part of man. But did you ever think about the risk that is demanded on God's part? In calling men into a covenant community, God took an enormous risk. He gave that covenant community a vocation: to create a climate in which love can evolve. He gave that covenant community a uniqueness: to be his co-creators of love. *Vocation* and *uniqueness* are the great and precious gifts of God. They are the gracious blessings of a loving Father. But they may also be insidious dangers. When a group of people realizes that it has a unique vocation it may have one of two responses: a joyous desire to share its gifts with the whole world or a selfish inclination to keep its gifts to itself. A covenant community, then, can be exclusive or inclusive. It can be particularistic or universalistic. The important thing is that, knowing this, God was willing to take a risk.

It was not very long before Israel was fumbling the ball. Increasingly she tended to see her uniqueness in terms of exclusiveness. Increasingly she began to see her vocation as making her a very particular people. God had called her to responsibility, to be a light to the whole world, but she had inverted his call to see it as a privilege, to keep the light to herself. Thus a new challenge was hurled at the covenant community, and once again the whole understanding of covenant relation was in danger. Was there someone who could meet this danger?

Fortunately for Israel, at this time in her history there was. The challenge was capably met by two theological traditions. One we know as the Yahwist School, coming from the Southern Kingdom. The other we know as the Elohist School, coming from the Northern Kingdom. These two theological traditions stressed Yahweh's covenant with Abraham, a covenant that includes and encompasses and goes out to all the world. Thus their thinking countered all conceptions of exclusiveness and particularity and privilege, and it insisted upon principles of inclusiveness and universalism and responsibility.

It did this in two ways: first, it said that the God of the covenant is also the God of the whole world. It is very difficult for us to grasp just how radical this is. In ancient thinking each nation had its own god, and he was confined to an area, a people, and a culture. That was taken for granted and no one even paused to consider whether or not that was the case. But Israel said, "No indeed, this is not so. Yahweh is the God of all creation, of all nations, of all societies. God's designs comprehend a great deal more than just Israel, than just the covenant community." This has always been terribly difficult for the whole world. It is quite easy, you see, to be unique *in* the world. The question is: How do you be unique *for* the world? It is quite easy to have a vocation *in* the world; but how do you have a vocation *for* the whole world? This is causing great tension in the contemporary church between those people who want the churches to be a cipher within society, and those people who are increasingly demanding that the church be the conscience of society. This rift is getting so deep that it is no longer just a tension. It is a division, and a necessary division.

Jesus had an insight into this problem. He told a story about a series of valleys. When the night would come there would be great darkness in the valleys, and the people who were stranded in the valley would have no way of finding where they were going. The world is like this. It is like a valley of night. People wander in it, and they do not know where they are going. But high on a ridge above those valleys there sits a city. Most cities, when darkness comes, shut their gates and man the watchtowers to protect themselves against the world that lies out there in the valleys. But there is something very different about this city. At night, when the darkness comes, this city high up on that hill throws open its gates and the watchmen who man the watchtowers call out into the valley, "Here we are. Come to the light. Find your direction. We light your way." There are many paths up out of the valley. No one path is special or particular. The only thing you have to do is climb. The gates are open and are ready to receive all who come.

Jesus said the covenant community is like this. Every stranger is welcome. There are some who want the covenant community to keep its light all to itself. They want to slam shut the city gates and fortify the battlements. Jesus told another story about a man who had a candle. Instead of holding that candle up to give his neighbor guidance, he took a bucket (and that is the proper translation: it is not a bushel) and he put the bucket over the candle. What happened? His light went out, and so did his life. Jesus said that this is not the nature of the covenant community. God's promise is to all men. The upward paths to the city may be many and varied. Which one is used is not crucial. The only critical issue is whether you are willing to make the climb. And all those who are willing are welcomed with open arms and received into the covenant fellowship. This keeps the covenant community humble and universal and inclusive and ethically responsible. The problem is, of course, that Christians have so often slammed and bolted the gates to the city. Even more than that, Christians have so often slammed the doors of their own houses and shut out not only their other neighbors, but also their fellow Christians. They have tried to keep their life to themselves and are quite willing just to leave the world in the darkness in which it exists.

This is the danger for any covenant community: that it

will mistake its uniqueness for exclusiveness, its vocation for privilege. And every covenant community must face this tension and this danger. It must discover how to maintain its unique vocation while at the same time being inclusive and universal.

The Yahwist and Elohist schools of theology also offered insight as to how this could be done. They said that to retain a sense of unique vocation and to maintain an attitude of universal inclusiveness demand two things—humble obedience and unconditional trust. At first glance these might seem like very pietistic kinds of things, but they are far from it. These are the demands of God on any community that is going to be in covenant. They stand opposed to all legalism, all codes, all commandments that are not based upon love, all rituals, and all dogmas. They support the ethic of love and the covenant relationship.

Jesus responded in these two ways: he was the totally obedient human being, and he was the unconditionally trusting man. Because of this, he gave a whole new definition to what it means to be a person, a human being. It is for this reason we call him Lord, or Christ. This is why we say, "He has fulfilled the law."

What is the response demanded from us today? To fulfill the law of Christ. What is the law of Christ? To create relationships of love, to become a covenant community, co-partners with God, evolving the ethic of love. How do we begin to do that? You may remember that in the book, *To Kill a Mockingbird*, the little girl, the daughter, comes and sits on her father's lap and asks, "Daddy, what is the meaning of compassion?" And the lawyer looks at her and thinks for a minute. He is defending a black man charged with rape. Finally he says, "Compassion means to get inside the other fellow's skin." The covenant community means to take responsibility for each other's lives. The terminology Jesus applied to it was "to bear each other's burdens." And Jesus as the Christ set the pace. He got inside our skins.

Who here is not lame and deaf and blind and guilty? Will

the person who is not lame and deaf and blind and guilty please stand up? No one stands, Christians, because we are all lame and deaf and blind and guilty. We cannot find among us a new Christ. But we can be like Christ to each other, and all together we can be the body of Christ. No man here can stand up on his own and say, "I am Christ." But together we can be the body of Christ. Christ shared our agony, and that is the meaning of the cross. So we are called to share each other's and the world's agonies. Vicarious suffering is not our fate; it is our *duty*. Burden-bearing is the office of Messiahship. Burden-bearing is the office of discipleship. If you expected Christ to bear your burdens, to get inside your skin, and if you are going to call yourself his disciple, that is what he expects of you. In its narrowest sense this means beginning with the person next to you. Look at him or her. That is where it begins. In its widest sense it extends to those who are our worst and deadliest enemies.

This is the Christian response to our unique vocation. Its dimensions are universal and inclusive. Its foundations are humble obedience and unconditional trust. This is the response of a covenant community. The path to the city on the hill leads through the agonies of the world. Vicarious suffering is not just the fate, but the duty of the covenant community, of the true Christian church. The church is called to bear the burdens of all humanity.

This means that as we go about our daily lives in an abundance of affluence, we must also feel the slowing pulse in the disease-ravaged hand of dying children; we must hear the ragged refugee in his stinking camp speak words of dark despair; we must be running for shelter with the horror-stricken father clutching his napalmed child to his own burned breast. Our hearts must be numbed with the fear of those who face death in the coronary care unit. Our souls must be empty with the loneliness of those who have sustained incredible loss in an airplane crash. We must be filled with the angry frustration of oppressed people who seek justice for their children in the ghettos of America. We must be there with the mother in the dead of night trying to keep the rats away from her children so they do not nibble their flesh. We must be numbed by the cold that chills the poverty-stricken rural poor who too often go to bed hungry.

This is the unique vocation God sets before his covenant community. It takes away all sense of exclusiveness, of particularity, of privilege. The office of the covenant community is to be the interceding and suffering church. Thus God opens his church out on the whole world. This unique vocation gives the covenant community a universal understanding. God saw this as so important that he was willing to take a risk then and now. Do we realize just how much of a risk God is taking on us? Do we dare to answer the dimensions of his risk?

## II. The Spontaneity of the Covenant Community

### Isaiah 1:10-17

When a human being develops a deeply personal relationship with another human being or with God or with both, a whole new dimension explodes into his life, the dimension of spontaneity, of being able to respond with the whole self, with all that is *you*. Perhaps this is the hardest thing in all of life to which we have to mature. How many of us feel unfettered, totally free, spontaneous (I do not mean to do ridiculous and inane things), to be ourselves, the people we are? Our social structure tries desperately to take this away from us, and our faith tries just as desperately to give it back.

Yahweh gave this spontaneity to Israel as part of her life as a covenant community, but Israel soon worked herself into a kind of religious *rigor mortis*. Her religion became an insistence upon codes and moralisms. Her worship became a cold repetition of rituals and forms. Her ethics became a performance of meaningless duties to God, not concern for fellow men. There was a strong reaction in Israel to this situation, and that reaction was provided by laymen. Amos was a layman and he said, "I hear Yahweh saying, 'I hate, I despise your feasts. I take no joy in your solemn assembly.'" Isaiah was a laymen and he heard Yahweh say, "Bring me no more offerings. They are an abomination to me."

This unyielding opposition of the prophets rocked Israel to her deepest foundations, and the issue was that of spontaneity within the covenant community. Ritualism had been turned into a lifeless routine of religious practice. Dogmatism had turned into a mechanical routine of religious thinking. What the prophets aimed to do was to reestablish the foundations of the covenant community. Israel had lost spontaneity, her ability to respond, both to God and to the needs of men. In other words, she had devalued her ethic until it was cheapened into an individualistic moralism. She had forgotten that the covenant community does not exist to think in conformity. The covenant community exists to respond spontaneously to God and the needs of men. And it can only do this when each person in the covenant community is responding to the needs of every other person. That is the new dimension of covenant living.

Jesus understood this. He had no interest in dogmas or rituals, and so he threatened the very roots of established religion. His only interest was in how men relate to each other and to God. If we really look at Jesus' life, we discover that it is a spontaneous response to human need; and it was through this response that Jesus rocked and rebuilt the covenant community. He restored its spontaneity. And it cost him his life.

How would Jesus respond to our contemporary churches—our contemporary covenant communities? Would he be overjoyed and support us, or would he come among us and be appalled and dismayed? Would he find spontaneity in our religious living, our worship together, our ethics, our ability just to respond to the needs of men? When was the last time you talked to another Christian about the deepest meanings of your life; not just as a friend to a friend, or a husband to a wife, but as a Christian to a Christian? When was the last time you looked another Christian directly in the eye? When was the last time you touched another Christian—not a handshake but a touch in which you knew that the whole faithfulness of the covenant community was at stake, dependent upon whether you did or did not touch that other person?

For me personally this is the hardest thing in the world

to do, to touch or be touched. I recoil from it. And yet I remember vividly the lesson that taught me the importance of what it means when Christians touch each other because covenant faithfulness is at stake. I was sitting in my office talking with a young woman who was—for good reason, not germane to my point here—deeply distraught and upset. My office is arranged so that the chair in which I sit is separated by a small coffee table from the couch on which my visitors sit. She was sitting there on that couch, choking and sobbing and literally writhing in her torment. It was obvious that her whole being, her whole self, was being spilled out in the open. Like a well-trained counselor I kept my distance. She sat on her couch and I sat in my chair. I watched while she agonized.

But there was something terribly wrong, because she needed more than just to sit there and spill herself out into the open with nobody really receiving except in a kind of detached and analytical way. All of a sudden it became quite clear to me that the whole covenant relationship, the whole human relationship, was at stake here. Suddenly I got up and walked over and sat down on that couch beside her. I reached up and put my hands on her shoulders, and she leaned down and laid her head on my shoulder and cried for an hour. Now the thing I learned at that point— and it is a tough lesson—is that there are times in our lives when the covenant relationship depends upon the human touch, or looking the other person in the eye, or the Christian-to-Christian exchange of meaningful words. But when were the last times any of these things happened to you?

These are substantive questions that must be answered by the covenant community. They go to the very heart of our existence, because they deal with our spontaneity. On our spontaneity hangs our ability to respond. On our ability to respond hangs our ethic. And on our ethic hangs our relationship to God. The prophets gave a clear answer to the covenant community. Jesus gave a clear answer to the covenant community. The question now is: Do we as Christians have a clear answer today? Are we fossilized in ritual and dogma? Or are we free to respond spontaneously to each other, to God, and to all humanity?

## 12. A Shepherd for the World

### Ezekiel 34

During the seventh and sixth centuries B.C. Israel's star had burned itself out. As political entities the Northern and Southern Kingdoms were burned-out meteorites. As a covenant community Israel was nothing more than a sputtering flicker. Yahweh had tried to lead his people as a shepherd leads his flock; and Israel had rejected his leadership.

Jeremiah, living in Jerusalem at this time, saw the break-up of the covenant community as inevitable. The reason was Israel's ingratitude and faithlessness, and the result was that the covenant relation would be taken away. Jeremiah says, "My eyes weep bitterly and run with tears because Yahweh's flock has been taken captive." Ezekiel, living in Babylon, saw himself in the midst of the breaking down of all the old and the building up of something very new. He said that faithlessness brings Yahweh's loving judgment, and that loving judgment is destruction. All the faults and oppressive institutions had to be eliminated. Thus both of the states, the Northern and Southern Kingdoms, had come tumbling down and the Temple had been leveled and destroyed. Now the question was: What would Yahweh do next? Would he simply cut Israel off and forget her and have nothing more to do with her?

Both Jeremiah and Ezekiel give a resounding "No" to that question. They said Yahweh would do three things. First, he would abrogate his role as Israel's shepherd. He would no longer himself be the shepherd of Israel. He would not perform that office in the world any more. Second, he would establish a new covenant with Israel and with all mankind. Jeremiah calls that new covenant the covenant of the heart; we discussed it in one of our earlier sermons. Ezekiel calls it the covenant of peace; we read about that in our Scripture. For both of them this new covenant was the gracious gift of Yahweh their God. For both of them the personal relation with Yahweh was based on the highest ethic imaginable.

The third thing that Yahweh would do—and this is in a way the most beautiful—was to send a shepherd. Jeremiah says, "I will gather the remnant of my flock and I will bring them back to their fold. I will set a shepherd over them, one who will care for them. Behold, the days are coming when I will raise up for the covenant community a righteous one, and he will deal wisely." Ezekiel envisioned this leader as one who would seek the lost and bring back the strayed and bind up the crippled, deliver the captives, strengthen the weak, watch over the strong, feed all the sheep on justice, judge between sheep and sheep, and make a covenant of peace.

This shepherd image is one of the most crucial symbols of Messianic hope. God will send one who will guide his flock. That one flock consists not only of Israel but of all the nations and peoples of the world. Jeremiah and Ezekiel then give the promise that Yahweh will send a shepherd and they give hope that this shepherd will bring a new covenant. It is this promise, plus this hope, that equals the expectation of the Messianic community: the hope that the Messiah would come; the anticipation, the expectation, that one would come to be a shepherd of the people.

Christians, of course, announced that this was fulfilled in Jesus. Here was the one whom Jeremiah and Ezekiel had anticipated. Here was the one whom the nations and Israel awaited. Here the promise, plus the hope, had been fleshed out into human form. And how does Jesus identify himself? He says of himself, "I am the good shepherd. The good shepherd lays down his life for his sheep. I know my own sheep and they know me. I have other sheep not of this fold. They also will hear my voice, so there will be one flock and one shepherd. I am the door of the sheep fold. Anyone who enters by me will be alive and will go in and out and find good pasture. He who does not enter by this door is a thief and a robber, and he will surely die; but he who enters by the door is a shepherd of the sheep. The sheep hear his voice, and he calls his own sheep by name, and he leads them in and out. He goes before them, and his sheep follow him, for they know his voice."

It was in these terms that Jesus announced his vocation as God's shepherd. He was to do what God's shepherd was to do. He was to seek the lost—and in our vision flashes the picture of Jesus reaching out and touching a leper or going to dinner with the Pharisee. He was to bring back the strayed—and in our vision flashes the picture of Jesus' deep concern over the rich young ruler. He was to bind up the crippled—and in our vision flashes the picture of Jesus concerned with the man with the withered arm. He was to deliver the captive—and in our vision flashes the picture of Jesus talking to the people about their bondage to the superstitions of their day. He was to watch over the strong—and in our vision we see the picture of Jesus conversing with Nicodemus. He was to feed all men justice—and the picture flashes through our vision of Jesus driving the money changers out of the Temple. He was to make a covenant of peace—and in our vision we see the picture of the Prince of Peace. Jesus did what the Good Shepherd, God's shepherd, was to do. He was totally obedient to his vocation. He fulfilled all the expectations, and because he fulfilled them he became the Messiah. (We use the word Christ; that is Greek for Messiah.)

What should we as part of the church, as members of the covenant community, celebrate at Christmas? Should our celebration be centered on the birth of Jesus or on his obedience? If it is centered on the latter the emphasis is taken off Christmas romanticism and placed on ethical responsibility. Most people, I am afraid, could not tolerate such a Christmas, and so, with the best intentions, they unwittingly support the paganization of the covenant community. But the covenant community understands Jesus' role as the Messianic shepherd. It is this group—perhaps only this group—that is aware of the true mystery of Christmas; a mystery not concerning birth, but obedience. Christmas is a time to celebrate the fulfillment of the Messianic expectation. It has to do with the very hard fact that Jesus fulfilled the office of shepherd. His reward for fulfilling that office was execution. Because he was ethically obedient he was killed. That is the meaning of Christmas. Who is prepared to celebrate that?

The execution of Jesus throws the whole Messianic expectation into chaos, for who now is to be a shepherd in the world? God has abrogated that office; Jesus is slain; and so the office of shepherd is vacant. Where, after the murder of Jesus, do we look for one who will be a shepherd? Who today fulfills the Messianic expectation? It is not God; he has removed himself from that office. It is not Jesus; he is dead. It is not clergymen; they are servants and apostles, but not shepherds. Who then is the shepherd in our day?

I think Paul staggers us with his answer. The Christian church, he says, is the body of Christ; and in it resides the Messianic expectation. The vocation of being the shepherd of the world belongs to the Christian community. Is this for the church an unnerving burden or a momentous joy? Is the reason for the lack of joy in contemporary churches that the churches have not accepted the vocation of shepherd?

What are the dimensions of that vocation? What does it mean that the covenant community is the shepherd of the world? What will it do? *Seek the lost.* Everywhere we go, Christians, we are confronting and confronted by bewildered people who are confused by life. Does the covenant community have the stability to provide insight and direction? *Bring back the strayed.* Our nation has gone terribly astray in its relations with other nations. Can the church bear enough witness to call our nation back? *Bind up the crippled.* Our society cripples its young people by demanding of them a conformity of which they want no part. Has the body of Christ enough balm to heal their wounds? *Deliver the captive.* Our heritage has disenfranchised the black man, the American Indian, the Puerto Rican, the Mexican American. Can the covenant community bring to bear enough influence so that these people can be set free in our lifetime? *Strengthen the weak.* The minds of our young people are churning with disenchantment and anger and hostility. Has the church enough patience to bear with them in their crisis? *Watch over the strong.* In the laboratories of our country men are discovering new ways to manipulate the destiny of the human race. Does the body of Christ have ethical insight to help guide that process? *Make a covenant of peace.* Here is perhaps the noblest risk of all. For there is no peace—not among the nations, not among the races, not among the generations. Could it be that there will be no peace in this world until the church finally accepts her vocation as shepherd?

Now if the Christian church were to accept fully the vocation of being shepherd to the world, how would it celebrate Christmas? Would it dwell on the birth of a baby born to a husbandless girl that became its mother? Or is that event really of peripheral concern? Should the Christian church not dwell instead on the birth of obedience in a faithful man? Is that not the event of maximum importance, an event that fleshes out God and gives meaning to our humanity? Jeremiah and Ezekiel never would have understood a group of people who went about splurging their resources over a miraculous birth. But they would have fully understood and shared with a faithful community that was celebrating its ethical obedience. They would have seen such a covenant community as celebrating its vocation of being the shepherd, and this for them would have been a mystery worth making a fuss about.

Every Christmas the Christian church has to face the

question: What are you making all that fuss about? The birth of a baby? That is a peripheral event, ethically neutral and very undemanding. Or are you making the fuss about the birth of obedience in Jesus the Christ? Does the church's celebration of Christmas remove religion from us and allow it to be on the periphery of a kind of pleasant time; or does it help us to understand that we hold the Messianic expectation in our hands? Does it help us to accept with joy and thanksgiving the vocation of being shepherds to a world that is out of the fold?

## 13. A Servant to the World

### Isaiah 52:13—53:12

Children are starving. Refugees are homeless. Black and Indian and Mexican Americans are ground into humiliation. Billions are spent on space exploration while the innermost parts of our cities rot away. Students are in revolt the world over. Our nation is plunged into meaningless war. The economy of the world is in crisis. The arms race continues. Yet we go about as Christians during Advent singing "Joy to the World." It is almost like comic relief.

I wonder if Christmas has become such a pagan ceremony because the world does not really take seriously the church and what it has to say about joy. It looks at the church and says, "What a joke you have tried to pull on us. We look around and see all this, and then we hear you sing 'Joy to the World.'" But I suggest that it is reasonable that we do so. And if it is reasonable, then what might we reasonably expect as the measure and dimension of the *joy* about which we sing?

Let us begin very simply. Joy means having someone who understands and accepts us for what we are, someone who will share our sorrows and griefs and sins, and, yes, our happiness and our pleasures. Joy means having someone who will show us the way of wholeness and humanness. We all know that we have turned off the right path—we do not have to be told that. But how desperately we need someone who will gently and patiently and firmly lead us back. And so we say, "Where shall we turn to find the Messiah for today?"

Isaiah gives the Messianic hope its most profound explanation. Potential joy for the world will reside first in the Servant of God. The Servant will be observed first as an individual. He will bear the griefs of mankind—all these things we have been talking about. He will carry the sorrows of humanity. He will be wounded for the sins of the faithless community, and he will be bruised for the errors of the nation. Humanity has turned aside from God's way. The Servant will be sent to lead humanity back—gently, patiently, and firmly. And joy will accrue to mankind because this Servant is willing to undergo this kind of pain and suffering. Thus joy for the world is purchased at a tremendously high cost to the Servant himself. Instead of being accepted and appreciated, he is abused and afflicted. What are the fruits of his travail? The covenant community is reconciled to God. Faithfulness is restored. The covenant community becomes one body. We understand that we are our brothers' keepers. The covenant community reaches out to all nations, races, and peoples. It becomes the light of the world. The covenant relation is no longer objective and impersonal, but our humanity, our humanness, depends upon how we relate to each other. This is the reasonable measure of joy we can expect from the world and from our faith.

Christians applied Isaiah's imagery of God's Servant to Jesus of Nazareth. He bore the grief of Mary and Martha over the death of Lazarus. Is this not the same grief that we all bear when a loved one dies? He carried the sorrows of a leper. Is this not the same hurt that we all feel when we know that we have in some way been socially ostracized? He absorbed the wounds of a mockery of justice. Is this not the same indignation that rises up within us when we know that our lives have been judged unfairly? And he opened himself to the bruising disaster of crucifixion. Is this not the same confusion that we feel today inside ourselves when evil executes all of the good intentions that we thought would bring so much beauty to the world and instead end in disaster?

How often we have discovered that we have wandered from the right path, and we yearn for someone who will patiently and gently guide us back. It is through suffering and pain that Jesus demonstrates the Way of Love. The personal cost to him to demonstrate for us what joy is was very high. It cost him his life. I think we really have to come to grips with the fact that Jesus, just like any one of us, wanted to be accepted and appreciated. Instead, he was afflicted and abused and finally executed. But what were the fruits of his adventure? What was the measure of his joy? He returned mankind to God; he reconciled us with the Father. He united all of us in one church; he reconciled us with each other. And he expanded our horizons to include the whole world; he reconciled us to the needs of all mankind. Jesus succeeded in making the covenant relation a very personal thing, and this was the measure of the joy of his life. He changed the ways that men thought and spoke and acted and related. He fulfilled the office of being God's Servant and he won the right to be called Messiah.

But Isaiah went on to say that this office of Servant would pass from an individual to a community of people faithful to the vocation of the Servant. This is exactly how the Christian church early identified herself. The mantle had fallen from Jesus onto the church, and the church's vocation was to fulfill the office of Servant in God's world. How? By sharing the griefs and the loss of loved ones, perhaps in death or divorce, or even in such a simple thing as the last child going off to school. By carrying the sorrow of those who are lost and isolated. By absorbing the wounds of those whose lives are frustrated, perhaps over a long illness, perhaps because a family is becoming unglued, perhaps because of old age, which makes them feel they do not have the energy they had before to do things they wanted to do. The trick is not to discover that the world about us is off the path—we know that. The trick is to find someone who will lead us gently, patiently, and firmly back.

Now here is the secret: the church has been led gently and patiently and firmly back by Jesus. The question is: Can the church apply in the world today what she has already experienced at the hand of her Lord? To demonstrate such depths of love will involve the church in pain and suffering, and the church, just like Jesus and just like any one of us, wants to be accepted and appreciated and approved (there are many churches willing to sell their souls for those things). The faithful church will be reviled and hated and scorned by those who claim to love her. She has no reason to expect otherwise. Isaiah tells us that. The life of Jesus tells us that. God is offering the church (here is the supreme Christmas gift) the opportunity to become his Servant. He places at its disposal all of his energy, all of his resources, and pleads with the church to use them to bring joy to the world so that joy will not be a joke or comic relief. But this opportunity God offers is a high-cost opportunity.

What would be the fruits of that adventure should we undertake it? Certainly reconciliation of our lives with God, certainly the supporting strength of the Christian family, certainly a sense of responsibility for the whole world in which we live. This is what the Christian can reasonably expect as the dimension of joy. Joy at Christmas is being called to the privilege of being Servant to each other. And beyond that, as we are servants to each other, being called together to the privilege of being Servant to the whole world. Then the measure of joy becomes clear. There are those who accept us for what we are, no strings attached. There are those who share our sorrows and our victories, our griefs and our pleasures, our pains and our joys. There are those who show us the way of wholeness and humanness. It is evident, is it not, that we have wandered from the path? But (and this is the trick of the gift again) we can show each other the way back. It is not the blind leading the blind. It is the Servant serving the servants. What a precious thing! No greater joy has any man than this, that he be God's Servant in the service of man.

So what shall Christians decide to celebrate at Christmas? The birth of a baby from the labor of an unwed mother? Certainly that is a good story. We should cherish it and praise it, enjoy it and celebrate it. But beyond that, what shall Christians (not just the secular world), what shall Christians truly celebrate at Christmas? The birth of a Servant church from the labor of Jesus who was called the Christ? It is not a very touching story. It is not a very fetching story. But it is joy to the world! Not comic relief, but real joy, for a world that desperately needs real joy.

## A Litany for Covenant Life

*Liturgist:* When you do it unto your brother you do it unto me.

*Choir:* Christian, can you feel the slowing pulse in the disease-ravaged hand of the starving child?

*People:* We do here covenant to heal the sick and feed the hungry.

*Liturgist:* When you do it unto your brother you do it unto me.

*Choir:* Christian, can you hear the ragged refugee in his stinking tent speak words of dark despair?

*People:* We do here covenant to clothe the naked and find good news for the hopeless.

*Liturgist:* When you do it unto your brother you do it unto me.

*Choir:* Christian, are you running for shelter beside that horror-stricken father clutching his napalmed child to his own burned breast?

*People:* We do here covenant to help the lame walk and bind up the wounds of the brokenhearted.

*Liturgist:* When you do it unto your brother you do it unto me.

*Choir:* Christian, is your heart numbed with the fear of those who face death or empty with the loneliness of those who have sustained loss in our hospital?

*People:* We do here covenant to succor the afflicted and comfort those who mourn.

*Liturgist:* Let justice roll down like waters, and righteousness like an ever-flowing stream.

*Choir:* Christian, are you filled with the anguished frustration of oppressed people seeking justice for their race and their children?

*People:* We do here covenant to set free the captives and release those who are bound.

*Liturgist:* Let justice roll down like waters, and righteousness like an ever-flowing stream.

*Choir:* Christian, are you weeping there upon that battlefield for those slain in a war that for them has no cause?

*People:* We do here covenant to be bearers of peace and reconcilers of enemies.

*Liturgist:* Let justice roll down like waters, and righteousness like an ever-flowing stream.

*Choir:* Christian, are you numbed by the cold that blows through the cracks of the backhill shack and chills the family of a man who has no work to do?

*People:* We do here covenant to lift up the poor and bring justice to the disenfranchised.

*Liturgist:* You are a chosen race, a royal priesthood, a holy nation, God's own people, that you may declare the wonderful deeds of him who called you out of darkness into his marvelous light.

*Choir:* Christian, do you feel the longing of a despairing and lonely world yearning for hope and joy and love?

*People:* We do here covenant to bring light and life and love into God's creation.

*All:* And what does the Lord require of us, but to do justice, to love steadfast mercy, and to walk humbly with our God. Amen.

# PART THREE

# THE INTERNAL LIFE
# OF THE COMMUNITY

# 14. The Covenant Community and the Social Order

*Micah 4:1-5*

One of the burning contemporary issues with which we have to grapple and about which we are anxious and confused is the issue of "law and order" and its relation to justice. The differing perspectives on this range from the extreme position that justice is nothing more than an outgrowth of law and order to the position that justice is the supreme issue with which we have to deal, and law and order must be made to conform to what is just.

If a community is going to exist, it must have structures to provide the discipline that makes the common life possible. The anarchical forces of our time have yet to learn this; and if they succeed in destroying the structures, they may learn a lesson of such chaotic proportions that it will provide disaster for us all. So the question of how structures are formulated is a matter of deep concern. What is the basic fabric of the social construct out of which we can live the common life? As we gather here as a people owning a covenant, we ask: Does the Christian faith have any insights to bring to bear on these kinds of questions?

We begin by searching out the perspective of Israel. If any people in the world ever discovered what it meant to live in covenant (even for a little while) Israel was that people. Israel was a people passionately devoted to social cohesion. They were preoccupied with disciplined living so that community could exist. The emphasis was on justice and order, and out of these grew laws to define that order. When we think of Israel's law, most of us think about the Ten Commandments. If you will read the prophets very carefully, however, you will find little mention of the Commandments as such. The emphasis on the Commandments reflects a breakdown of law and order, and, most important, of justice. Micah does not talk about law and order in terms of the Ten Commandments. He talks about it in terms of loving mercy, doing justice, and walking humbly with your God. People turned to the Commandments when justice was dead. I think it is important for us not only to be aware of this but to ask whether that is the precipice on which we totter in our contemporary life? If in our society justice and law and order (in the Israelite understanding of those words) die, then we shall see a reaction that will give us nothing better than the Ten Commandments, and Jesus makes it clear they are not enough.

What the Israelite law does is provide a whole new dimension in human history. We can compare it to the legal systems of other ancient peoples, and we will see much that seems similar at first sight. But when we look at Israelite law closely, we will find—underneath the superficial similarities with other legal codes—that it is one of the most magnificent things that ever happened in human history. Israel provides a mutant in the ordering of human life. Because of her understanding of justice and law and order, human life took a whole new direction.

It is difficult for us to grasp the radical change Israel created. There were four elements in this new understanding of law and order and justice: first, disciplined determination to relate the whole of life obediently to the will of God; second, the fashioning of a social order that is a demonstration of the will of God; third, the idea that man is not a thing but an extension of divine reality; fourth, the notion that human life is based on a humanitarian spirit that sets men free to be fully human. Thus justice raises the question: What makes man human? Order raises the question: What structure can be created to allow for humanness? And law raises the question: What discipline will provide these structures for the community? That is what Israel brought to human understanding.

But how does this work out practically? We could take an example from Israel's life and use that, but that would be somewhat removed, so let us instead take an example from our own lives, from the ordering and structures of our own society. Let us ask: How does this work out practically? A public school district is facing a crisis with regard to the salaries of teachers. There are all kinds of questions raised in this dispute. How will it affect the tax base of the whole economy of the community? What about the statistics that both parties put forward—sometimes they seem different? Who is correct? What is the public readiness to accept increases in teachers' salaries? What about the use of sanctions by the teachers? What about the possibility of unionization by the teachers? And we can go on and on with important and crucial questions that need to be asked.

All of these are reasonable questions, and they must be addressed. But I suggest that there is a whole other level of questions that must be raised from a Christian perspective. Not that those I have just mentioned are unimportant, but it is the responsibility of the Christian community to dig down below the immediate questions to what might be called the foundation questions, the questions upon which the immediate questions rest. Here is one: Are we willing (or even able) to see in the teachers' struggle a relationship to our obedience to the will of God? Here is another: Are we seeking ways of fashioning for our teachers a social order that will be a demonstration of God's intent for them as human beings? A third question: Are we treating our teachers as things or as extensions of the reality of God? A fourth question: Are we setting our teachers free to discover the maximum dimensions of their humanness?

Beneath all the practical questions the Christian begins to ask questions like these. They are much more difficult, because they do not deal with money but with humanness.

They are much more basic because they are finally determinative of what we expect for our children and our community, but most important for the humanness of the teachers among us. These questions are not concerned with taxes. They are concerned with justice and order and law from a Christian point of view. Are we sensitive to the humanness of our teachers? That is the question of justice. Are we creating structures in which they can work out their humanness? That is the question of order. Are we providing a social discipline by which these structures can be created? That is the question of law.

Every community fashions for itself a certain kind of socio-economic cultural situation. Many communities have created an environment in which those who work for the people of the community cannot live among them. This is the bind in which many people find themselves—teachers, nurses, nonprofessional employees of colleges and hospitals—they must live outside the town where they work. The result of this is a sense of not belonging to the community for which they have responsibility. This has vast social implications. It says a great deal about our sensitivity to the humanness of those we expect to work for us. It says an enormous amount about our attitude toward justice and law and order when these are viewed from a Christian perspective.

Jesus defined a unique perspective that made clear the issue that Israel raised. Jesus said law equals *love*. That is it—law equals love. Order equals a *new humanness*. And justice equals the *new humanness demonstrating love*. He lived out this understanding in his own lifetime. And he gave the church the burden and the joy of living it out after his death. In our day the church is doing an increasingly better job of living it out. The fact that we can raise these kinds of questions in the church is an indication of that. The church is asking the right questions beneath the obvious ones. The church is holding up the processes of humanness and saying, "Look at them." And the church is demanding that the deeper questions of being human be taken seriously. The gift of God is the insight to address these to the meaning of being human. And the glory of the covenant community is to use this gift in every situation no matter how complex. Can we, as Christians, bring the insights, the gifts of God, the order, the law, and the justice of Israel to bear on the socio-economic situations we see around us? That is the question of how the covenant community addresses the social order.

## 15. The Covenant Community and the Person

*Jeremiah 1:4-10*

In the preceding sermon we looked at Israel's self-understanding as a society, particularly in relation to issues of justice, law, and order. Now we turn to look at Israel's understanding of the individual within that social construct. Jeremiah has often been called the prophet of *individualism*, though he certainly had no concepts that would parallel our American ideal of "rugged individualism." But he did have incisive insights into the purpose and place of the individual within the covenant community.

Let us investigate two differing perspectives on the existence of the individual, the individual's place in the social order, and God's relation to the individual. The first viewpoint might be referred to as the pervasive "Western" perspective, commonly identified as "Christian." The second viewpoint is the perspective of that covenant community called Israel, and the context out of which Jesus of Nazareth lived his life.

| GOD IS THE PROTECTOR OF THE INDIVIDUAL | GOD IS THE CREATOR OF HUMANNESS |
|---|---|
| 1 | |
| Man defines his own values. He sees the determination of what is right and wrong as his role. | God is understood as "person." He defines the dimensions of personhood. Man moves toward the fulfillment of personhood (traditionally called "godliness"). |

2

God is expected to support and protect what man has determined to be of value.

God becomes the pattern of all human goodness, and man derives his values from this pattern.

3

"It is my right to own property. I do own property. It is God's task to protect my right to own property."

"God owns my life and all that I dare call 'mine' is *his*. He gives me everything as his steward. My task is to use it in his service."

4

The expression of the individual life is *externalized*, so that existence is seen as relationship to *things*.

The individual expresses his existence as an *internalized* relationship to the personhood of God.

5

Concern centers upon individual rights, property, and the preservation of things.

Concern expresses itself in justice, order, and law as defined by the personhood of God.

6

The emphasis is upon *rules*, which are externalized codes of social behavior.

The emphasis is upon *people* and their struggle to become "persons."

7

The individual in society is judged on the basis of his conformity.

The individual is always recognized as a participant in God's action of creating "persons."

8

The individual is constrained by those externalized forms (morals) impinging upon him.

The individual is set free through the internal creation of his own and others' personhood.

9

The important groups for the individual to identify with include property owners, people of the highest social strata, members of the power structures, pietistic moralists, the "good" people.

The critical groups to identify with are the disenfranchised, the poor, the underprivileged, the stranger, the alienated minority, the enslaved, the victims of war, etc.

10

Social awareness is defined in terms of "what is good for *me.*"

Social awareness becomes "how can I participate in God's process of creation to develop personhood in others through myself."

11

Life is ordered on the basis of what will benefit the individual or his group.

Life is ordered on the basis that it will reveal the will and love of God for other human beings.

12

The individual lives under an imposed duty to compulsory regulations.

The individual lives out of a *personal decision* to allow his life to be a revelation of the dimensions of personhood and love.

13

Living is grounded in pragmatic rationalism.

Living becomes an expression of personhood based upon a covenant with God and neighbor.

14

The primary stimulus is "do not break the rules."

The primary stimulus is "love God and my brother."

**15**

The individual is bound to the past and his potential to develop his humanness destroyed.

The individual is released to adventure into the future to discover the dimensions of his humanness.

**16**

The individual's *obligation* is to "keep" (preserve and defend) man-made structures and definitions (morals).

The developing person rejoices in *obedience* to God's Way of Love.

**17**

This obligation results in *legalism*.

This obedience results in *self-surrender*.

**18**

Rules, codes, morals become the directors (authority) of life.

God's Way of Love becomes the single director (authority) of life.

**19**

Relationships are grounded in an essential distrust of other humans.

Relationships become an acting out of recognition of common human need.

**20**

This distrust destroys community.

This acting out creates community.

**21**

The individual becomes an obedient *creature* out of his *fear*.

The individual becomes an obedient *person* out of his *joy*.

**22**

This fear diminishes the worth of the individual and pushes him toward a sub-human level.

This joy expands the worth of the individual and pushes him toward fulfillment of his personhood.

23

The individual becomes directed towards things (rules, status, property, etc.).

The *developing person* becomes directed toward developing persons (his neighbor and even his enemy!).

24

This direction diminishes life to the level of frustration and chaos.

This direction raises life to heights of love and creativity.

25

The individual's driving force is his lust for power and possessions.

The person discovers his life exalted in direct ratio to his involvement in the needs of others.

26

All other human beings become *things*.

All other humans become *extensions of God's personhood.*

27

The ultimate end is *law* for the sake of preserving the individual's isolation from other individuals.

The ultimate end is *love* for the sake of losing one's isolation within the community, thus expanding the potential of personhood in one's self and others.

28

The ultimate result is that freedom, humanness, and personhood are destroyed. (This condition of human existence has traditionally been called: "Hell.")

The ultimate result is that freedom, humanness, and personhood are fulfilled, and God's creation is completed. (The traditional terms for this condition are: "Kingdom of God," "Heaven.")

## 16. The Covenant Community
## and Its Cultic Expressions

### Psalm 97

At the center of life there is a mystery. There are various cryptograms to describe that mystery. One of those cryptograms is G-O-D. The word itself—the particular combination of sounds pronounced "God"—has no intrinsic value. It is merely a symbol for the mystery that lies at the profoundest depths of human existence. We do not even know what we mean when we utter the word "God." It is no more than a symbol for our lack of ability to grasp that which we know is at the heart of our existence. There are some who have sought to use different code words. Paul Tillich calls this mystery "the ground of our being." He does not use the word God. Emil Brunner speaks of the "Energy of Love." Israel too had a word, a cryptogram. It was "Yahweh," and it was translated, "I am." No more than that—just "I am." That was the name of God.

The point is that whatever symbolic words we use, they all express one thing, and that is the veiled mystery—unable to be grasped or seen—at the very heart of life. And anyone who does not think that God is the deepest, most profound mystery at the heart of life is simply fooling himself.

Now when the path of our life is crossed by the path of the Eternal Mystery, that is worship. It may occur—and this is deeply important for Christians—at any time and at any place. It may be participated in by the atheists who deny that the mystery even exists. It is not something reserved for Christians. Worship is the potential reality contained within every moment of every human existence. Wherever love is created, there worship occurs. By whomever love is created, that person is at worship.

One mode of worship, and only one mode of worship, is the cultic act of the covenant community of faith. Beginning in the days of Abraham, Israel (and the church as the extension of Israel) set aside special times for the cultic act of worship. In this deliberate cultic act in which we engage, the community celebrates the potential of worship in the life of every person. So what the community does is to gather consciously to stand in the presence of the Eternal Mystery. Cultic worship—very deliberate, very conscious— is why we gather together on the Lord's Day. We come first to stand present to the Eternal Mystery before the world; and second, to declare publicly the intentions of the covenant community. Thus the covenant community very deliberately orders its cultic expressions.

What are the essential elements of worship in the church? What are the cultic expressions? There are three. First, the church gathers to declare before the world the story of the mighty acts of God. This story begins with creation, goes on to the Exodus, to Jesus the Christ, to the church, and on to this very day, to God's people who exist in this place at this time. We are part of the drama God unfolds before the world. We are part of his mighty acts. This *day* is a mighty act of God. If you do not believe that, just think that you might be dead today. You have been given a *day!* That is a mighty act of God. That day could be taken from you. You may have never awakened this morning; but you did, and that is a mighty act of God! What this does is to get straight the human intercourse with the mystery at the heart of being. It impresses on man a deep sense of his creatureliness. At the same time it explodes the potential of the dimensions of humanity. You have a day, a whole day, in your hands to use. What will you do with it? You see, God has acted, and because he has acted man is forever different. Because you woke up this morning you are different, for you could be dead. But you are not; you are alive! So you are different. Now what Israel, the church, does is to gather together to celebrate these mighty acts of God and declare them before the world.

The second thing the church does is to declare before the world the story of how the covenant community lives out the faith. The church's foundation is the story of the mighty acts of God. Now this story causes the church to act and react, to live in a specific way. The church is a living demonstration of what God intends mankind to be. Often in talking with someone about the church I have said, "But that is not the way the church ought to be." Sometimes the reply I hear is, "You are just naive; that is the way the world is." To which the only answer is, "Yes, that is the way the world is; but you are the one who is naive, because the church is made to be different than the world is." That is the whole rationale for its existence, and Christians have not gotten that through their heads yet. The church is made to be different from the world. It is a living demonstration of what the world ought to be. When the church is less than that, it is not living out of the mighty acts of God. Now what the church wants to do is to tell the story of how it does live out the mighty acts of God. Its cultic worship becomes a public expression of the community life pattern. Worship is the story of the way a Christian lives his life.

So we have two stories. One is the story of the mighty acts of God, and the other is the story of how the community lives out those acts. The third element of worship brings these two together. The church gathers to hold these two stories up to the whole world. God's mighty act of love is for all mankind, and nobody is excluded. Now the problem is that the world does not realize or accept this. Therefore, what the Christian community does is to come together to rehearse these stories for the world, and it does that over and over again, at least fifty-two times a year.

You see what worship is: it is God's commercial that keeps interrupting the program of life. God buys the time of the world; we did not put it there. God bought it. It is his program. What he does—just as anyone has experienced who has watched a movie on television—is to keep interrupting the program with his commercials. Worship is God's commercial. It keeps reminding the people who are involved in the program and watching the program that they are not paying for it. God is. Some people react as angrily to God's commercial of worship as we do to the commercials that break the thread of the televised movie. But that is what he is doing: interrupting life to tell us who is really paying for what is going on.

The task of the church is to keep presenting this commercial—these two stories—to the world. Thus, those of you who worship represent all those people who stay home in bed. You are in church for them. You are there for everyone who hates the faith and hates his brother, for all the atheists and all the unbelievers. It is a fantastic and overwhelming burden and a fantastic and overwhelming joy.

But, you see, this means that worship is very objective. We are here to engage in a task, a duty. The cultic worship of the Christian community is a task done by Christians for the whole world. This may make us a little anxious. We wonder about subjective feelings. Should we not "feel" a "religious experience" in our worship? Many people are uptight about this. If they do not feel a subjective religious experience from worship, they think something is wrong. The truth is that subjective feelings and experiences are strictly secondary to the cultic worship of the church. If they come during the time of worship, well and good. If they do not come, that too is fine; that is not what we are worshipping for. This is not to say that all feelings of religious experience in life are illegitimate. Certainly not. Religious feelings and experiences in life are the most legitimate things that can happen to us. But—and this is the crux of this sermon—religious feeling should occur as we exercise love in our daily lives. This is the arena of religious experience: daily life, seven days a week, twenty-four hours a day.

The most profound religious feelings and emotions come because of what we do in love for other people, and what we receive in love from other people. If religious experience does not come at those points, then we are not truly religious people. Anyone who comes to a church service and expects to have happen there what is not happening to him in his daily life simply does not know the score. What we gather for is to celebrate in community the religious experiences that have happened to us all week long. Religious experiences do not occur in church (though at times they may); *celebration* occurs. We gather to celebrate what has occurred in our daily life, to tell our stories of how God's mighty acts have shaped our lives. We gather to celebrate the worship we have been doing. We come to demonstrate how our lives have been crossed by that Eternal Mystery. In celebrating these stories we make the world conscious of the presence of the Divine Mystery. And that is our task in cultic worship: to hold forth to the world the stories of God and the stories of our lives. And then to celebrate. No more than that, but no less!

## 17. The Covenant Community and Its Mode of Communication

### Jeremiah 15:10-21

I recently read an article in a national news magazine entitled "Can Modern Man Pray?" Various insights were offered by renowned religious leaders ranging from Roman Catholics to Quakers. They all agreed that prayer, as it is commonly described and used in our religious definitions, has no validity for the contemporary man.

Certainly prayer is one of the most elusive, ambiguous, confusing aspects of our religious life. What is it? How does it work? Why does it so often seem so empty? Is it no more than a projection of our own desires, a kind of autosuggestion? Has prayer too slipped from our grasp in the chaos of the twentieth century? God knows we need it. When the path of our lives is crossed by the path of the Eternal Mystery we need something, but what is it we need? I would suggest to you that our most profound need as human beings is an adequate prayer life. Both as individuals and as a corporate community we need it; as persons and as a church. At the heart of our existence as Christians, if there is no prayer, then we have nothing.

I would like to begin by suggesting that we can describe prayer on two levels: static prayer and dynamic prayer. Static prayer, it seems to me, has countless manifestations. It might take the form of a desire to conjure from God the substance of our own wishes. Or it might take the form of personalistic piety in which we congratulate ourselves on our particular attributes. Another form it takes is a meritorious humility ("I, Lord, I am the sinner") designed to curry divine favor. Or it might be an attempt to lose the self in the divine infinity through contemplation and thus not have to deal with anything. Some people use it as a retreat to avoid the task of having to live. Others enjoy rigidly prescribed formulas as if these will arouse the divine interest and somehow stimulate God to take an interest in their lives. Or there is the kind of formal cultic trumpery, the embellishment of the trappings of religion.

We could go on and on with other descriptions. I think you know what I mean by static prayer. Isaiah said, "When you spread forth your hands in prayer, I will not listen; for your hands are full of blood, and I will not hear from bloody hands." You notice it was not from the mouth that Yahweh heard the prayer; it was from the bloody hands. Amos said, "I hate and I despise your worship. I take no delight or joy in your solemn assembly. Take your prayers away from me. I will not listen to them, for you are a guilty people." Again it is not the words of the mouth, but the guilt of social relations. The Judeo-Christian tradition has always stood staunchly against this kind of prayer. It springs from a kind of religion in which man creates God in his own image and then prays in self-congratulation. Most of the religions of the world (and, in my experience, many Christians) operate out of this kind of orientation.

Israel had a different perspective on man's relation to God. Israel said, "God is the Creator and man is created in God's image." This relationship gives quite a different dimension to prayer. Prayer is seen as the interaction of man with God on the deepest levels of human existence. For Israel prayer was the dynamic *experience* of living with God in your guts. Prayer was at the very center of what it means to be a human being. Thus prayer arose out of the elements that constitute human life.

What are those elements that really make up life? If you had to list the five things that really constitute life, what would they be? I suggest to you these five. First, our goofs: the rebellion against our own humanness; our hostility and ingratitude; our pleasant, pleasant viciousness; our loving spitefulness; our stupid mistakes that cause other people so much trouble; our intentional irascibility that creates a friction we rather enjoy. Second, our joy: the joy for a new day given and the joy for being alive on this day; of being able to come and share with our fellow Christians the celebration of the worship we have been doing all week; for the gracious and the good and the loving things that do happen to us in our lives. Third, our personal need: our frustration, anxiety, and fear, our temptation to be less than we are, and, perhaps most dangerous of all, our unwillingness to accept ourselves. Fourth, our relationship with others: sometimes it is good, sometimes it is lousy; but often it is a real recognition of the needs of other people and a desire to help. And fifth, our gratitude for all that makes all of living worthwhile, just pure and simple gratitude.

These, I would suggest, are the essential ingredients of every human life. Goofs, joys, needs, relationships, and gratitude. Now we can deal with all of those alone, by ourselves. We can shut all others out—both men and God— and deal with those five elements of life in utter isolation. "I am the Puritan man, able to handle myself." What nonsense, but we can try! And there are a lot of people who do just that. They keep the dimension of life little. They encompass themselves within a shield that nobody can penetrate, and life becomes a very little thing.

But there is an alternative. We can also deal with these five elements of life in conjunction with God. We can open the innermost recesses of our lives. We can shatter the shield and let God in. And the person and the community who are living out of a covenant seek to do this—to expand the dimensions of life by sharing with God and man all that happens in the innermost recesses of life. In this situation the experiences of life become the life of prayer. Our goofs are the living out of our confessions. Our joys are the living out of our praise. Our personal need is the living out of our petition. Our relationships with others are the living out of our intercession. Our gratitude is the living out of our thanksgiving. When we allow God to *be* at the very center of our daily existence, we have a life of prayer. Prayer talked about in this way is the life style out of which we live our public and our personal lives. How we live is how we pray. Our life, personal and corporate, is our prayer.

Does this mean, then, that we do not need formal prayers? Indeed not! Formal prayers now become exceedingly important. When prayer is understood in the way we have described, formal prayers are necessary. Israel early developed formal prayers based on the elements of life. Celebration hung upon the ingredients of being human. Thus the flow of private and corporate worship was always *confession* and *praise* and *petition* and *intercession* and *thanksgiving*. Christians have maintained that flow as the essential elements for constructing our celebration. The covenant community (be it Hebrew or Christian) recognizes the need for two types of prayer—formal, personal prayer used daily to support the person, and cultic prayer used publicly to support the community.

But, one may ask, if prayer is a stance of life, why are formal prayers necessary? Why is it even necessary to come and gather in celebration? Let us try this analogy, remembering that, like any analogy, it has its limitations. Formal prayer is the recipe book for living. Now no one is going to make a complicated gourmet cuisine without a recipe to insure the proper blending of the ingredients. This proper blending assures a delicious taste to the finished product. Similarly, life is a complicated gourmet delight. What we need is a recipe to tell us how to properly get in all the ingredients that are needed, how much and how to balance them. Without the recipe life is tasteless and flat and unappetizing. With the recipe life is superb and delicious and magnificent. What formal personal and public prayer does is *give us the recipe for living*. It tells us how to put the ingredients together properly.

There are some people who feel that if they do not have some kind of emotional experience inside of them when they read a prayer, they are not praying. And yet those same people, if they go to a recipe book and read a recipe, do not expect to taste anything in their mouths from reading the recipe. But you must have a good recipe if you are going to have good food. Personal and cultic prayers are the same thing. They are not necessarily going to give you any great stimulation inside. But what they give you is the recipe out of which life ought to be lived, and the flavor comes when you put them all together and live your life that way. Life's flavor depends on how the recipes are used.

So the order of adequate prayer life goes something like this: Formal personal and cultic prayers are used regularly. Personal prayers are used every day, morning and evening, in private. Cultic prayers are used as often as the community gets together. These provide the ingredients for devout life. They tell us how it is put together. Then the covenant life is lived with God at the very center, and this living is the mixing of the ingredients together. Thus the flavor of life depends on faithfully fulfilling the recipe. The whole life style of the believer fulfills his prayer. How he lives is how he prays. His life is his prayer. I would suggest that in terms such as these we can answer the question "Can modern man pray?" with a resounding affirmative. Yes, modern man can pray; and yes, many modern men are doing a devout and very good job of it.

# A Litany for Covenant Life

*Liturgist:* The Lord reigns; let the earth rejoice!

*People:* Christian, my prayer for you is that you will have the gifts of Christ; joy and freedom and hope that will make our tired world inspired again; commitment and vision and single-mindedness so that through your life a weary humanity may be renewed.

*Liturgist:* The Lord loves those who hate evil; he preserves the lives of his saints; he delivers you from the hand of the wicked!

*People:* Christian, my prayer for you is that we may enter into such depths of human communion that because of our fellowship a world that exists by competition may learn that its survival depends on cooperation, and that nations that live by war may understand that life exists only in peace.

*Liturgist:* Light dawns for the righteous, and joy for the upright in heart!

*People:* Christian, my prayer for you is that you may so live that through your life the discontent of the young, the rebellious, and the prophetic may be made holy and consecrated, so that through their lives may come justice, brotherhood, and dignity for all mankind.

*Liturgist:* The Lord loves those who hate evil; he preserves the lives of his saints; he delivers you from the hand of the wicked!

*People:* Christian, my prayer is that you will have the power of the Spirit to relieve and succor those weak in body and mind; those depressed in spirit and enduring pain; those who are confused by a changing world; those who are dying physically, mentally, or spiritually; and that you may give of yourself strength and aid unto them.

*Liturgist:* Light dawns for the righteous, and joy for the upright in heart!

*People:* Christian, my prayer for you is that you will shower the great love of God on all who feel themselves outcast, alienated, disenfranchised, imprisoned, lonely, or forgotten; so that all whom you meet on your daily round may be given through you a full measure of the humanness flowing from our Elder Brother, Jesus the Christ.

*Liturgist:* Rejoice in the Lord, O you righteous, and give thanks to his holy name!

*People:* Amen!

*Liturgist:* Amen!

*All:* Amen!

PART FOUR

# THE NATURE OF THE COVENANT GOD

## 18. The Covenant God Gives Personhood

### Exodus 3:7-14; 4:1-16

When parents bring home their new child, what is it that they most anticipate about that child, about his life, about what will happen next? I suggest that the most critical dimension of that new child's life—surely the one most anticipated by his parents—will be the first word he speaks. The first step he takes is important, but the first word he speaks will move him from one level of being to a whole new level of being, because, for the first time, the parents and the child can communicate on the level of language. There has been communication before, but the promise of language is a promise that the whole internal life of that being can be opened up and made known. I suggest that this is what parents really await, the opportunity to know that child in the innermost recesses of his being, to know who he really is. Language is the promise of that knowledge. The child becomes identifiable as a person, not just as an individual any longer, but as a person through his words, his language.

Our aim in these next sermons will be to try to discover how we can talk about the nature of the God whose path crosses our paths. When we begin to talk about that, all our talk must begin with the statement that God is personal. That is where all Judeo-Christian thinking about the nature of God begins—with the affirmation that he is personal. But what do we mean by that in the world in which we live? For most world religions God is an impersonal force, a cosmic force of nature that impinges upon us or removes himself from us. The whole construct of twentieth-century thought is aimed at depersonalizing everything that we come in contact with, including other human beings and God. Still, Judeo-Christian theologians have wrestled with this problem of the personhood of God as with no other problem. There have been literally millions of words and thousands of volumes written to explain it, and I confess that the ones I have read carry minimal meaning for me. I have not yet been able to grasp fully what they mean when they talk about the personalness of God. And yet it is an understanding that cannot be lightly set aside, because that personalness is so much a part of us that it would be like saying that love does not exist to say that God is not personal. So we must address the question: What do we mean when we say that God is personal?

Israel, the covenant community of the Old Testament, sought to verbalize her understanding of what she meant by this, and her understanding was summarized in this potent Scripture passage where Moses has a conversation with Yahweh. By revealing his name, Yahweh chooses to be definable, distinctive, and personal. The Eternal Mystery chooses to pull aside the veil. Thus Israel stands against all abstract concepts of God. She will not tolerate any philosophical understanding of him. And Israel stands against any nameless cosmic force. She will not tolerate any mystical understandings of him. The Eternal Mystery at the heart of being comes forth from the heart of that being and shows himself. He offers himself in fellowship with men. He gives men access to himself. He opens himself and says, "I am concerned about the lives of my children."

Read that again: "I hear their call of suffering. I will go down and deliver them." He cares, but in his caring he will have his way. Notice how Moses tries to say, "Yahweh, send somebody else but don't send me." And Yahweh says, "You will go." He will have his way in shaping individual and social life. He demands the submission of human will to his intention. And he makes human community his goal. Thus, what he is really saying is that the human being has no escape from the nearness of the Eternal Mystery. The psalmist calls it "the close overbrooding shadow." God passionately demands the life of every human being, and his goal is that human community be the goal of every human life. Yahweh is a person, and all individuals move from being individuals to becoming persons (to becoming truly human beings) by understanding that the goal of their life is the goal of his life—that human community exist. This is no philosophical deism, but it is the dreadful presence of the Eternal Mystery at the heart of our being, pulling aside the veil. For Israel this was a profound joy.

But I suggest that for most of us who live in the latter part of the twentieth century Israel's answer is insufficient. I would also suggest that the answers of all the theologians are insufficient. I have been searching for something to help us today in understanding what we mean when we say that God is personal. We have to deal with this question. In the face of Israel's answer and the answer of all the theologians, I make no pretense that this suggestion will be sufficient.

The cue comes from two sources: first, from the child, who demonstrates his personhood by his ability to speak; and second, an insight from a theologian by the name of Hans Urs von Balthasar. Let me reiterate that we recognize the being of the child as personal when we begin to grasp the promise that is held in his first words of communication. Now we begin to see that that child's innermost mystery will indeed be open to us, and we can search it out and know it. The fact that the human speaks reveals that he is a personal being. Words are the declaration of our personhood. Now turn to the theologian, von Balthasar. He calls man the "language of God." Putting these two together, the child and the theologian, we could then say: God is known to us as personal because he speaks words to all humanity through each person.

God has a language we can hear. In Christian theology Christ has always been called the Word of God. We say we know the being of the Eternal Mystery because Christ is the Word to the world, and that is true. But there is more to it than just that. We know (and this is the crux of what I am trying to say) the being of the Eternal Mystery because *every single human life is the word of God* to the world. Our lives collectively and your life specifically is the word of God. You are the language in which God communicates to the world. In every human life we hear the voice of God.

Now we have a remarkable situation on our hands. God is known as personal because you exist. This means that he can be no abstract concept unless you are an abstract concept—and who will define himself as an abstract concept? This means that God is no philosophy, unless you are a philosophy! Is there one among us who defines himself as a philosophy? This means that God is not a nameless cosmic force, unless you are a nameless cosmic force! Is there a nameless cosmic force among us? My point is this: through you and because of you God shapes the destiny of human existence. Through you and because of you God is evolving the goal of humanity which is community.

You see, there is no escaping the overbrooding nearness of the Eternal Mystery, because—whether you like it or not—God is speaking through your life. Passionately, God is speaking through your life. You are the word of God to the world of men. The language that God speaks is the style of your life. We may react to this in many ways. We may rebel. We may fight God. We may be indifferent. We may be simply bored. Or we may rejoice and be glad. And I submit to you that this is the Christian response: to rejoice and be glad that we are the language of God to the world of men. Jesus reacted with total joy and therefore we call him the Christ. To continue our analogy, we might say that Jesus is the dictionary of God's language. He contains all the words, and each word's reality is explained in him. But that is what he is, the dictionary, and the dictionary is no longer a spoken word. The dictionary is not a language. When you pick up the dictionary you do not hear language.

There is no way out, you see. You are the language. You are the spoken word. This is no vague deism, but the dreadful presence of the Eternal Mystery. This is no impersonal force, but God talking to the world because you exist. I know that God is personal because I hear him through your existence. Indeed God is a very personal being, so personal that in your life style his word is spoken to the world. Rejoice and be glad. You are God's language.

## 19. The Covenant God Gives Spirit

*Isaiah 57:14-21*

As human beings we are capable of experiencing and reflecting on many phenomena. Who has not experienced at the center of his or her being the phenomenon of the power of energy—a mysterious unknown presence that moves us when we cannot move ourselves, when we are so set against something that we are determined not to be moved, and yet we are moved? And who is not aware that this energy is completely other than human? It exists beyond us. We do not create it. It may move us, but we are not responsible for the energy itself. Or who can remain long unaware that this same energy pervades the whole existing order? We can at times sense it within ourselves, shaping, creating, molding our lives; but we can also sense it in the lives of other human beings, or in the newborn child, or at times even in the animal. And I would suggest to you that for the truly sensitive person it can be sensed also in the rock or the tree or the pulsar.

This energy knits the universe together. Subatomic material becomes atoms. Atoms become molecules. Molecules become cells, out of cells come plants and animals and man, and out of man comes society. A driving energy, a pervasive power, seems to be knitting all our lives together. We experience this tendency in all things, from the most basic stuff of the universe to our own interpersonal relations. Everything is seeking to converge. The energy is pushing all of the stuff of the universe to unity and coherence. And who can doubt, if you have experienced

these things, that this energy is moving relentlessly forward? I suggest to you that this describes a phenomenon
which we can and do experience as human beings.

It also describes what the Christian means when he says:
God is Spirit. The spiritual nature of God is not a philosophical concept, but an experience of the phenomena
that surround us in the world if we are only sensitive to
them. The Christian has a special technical language to
describe this. For the word "energy," the Christian uses
the word "God." For the complete otherness of this energy, the Christian uses the phrase "the holiness of God."
For the total pervasiveness of this energy, the Christian
uses the phrase "the transcendence of God." And for the
dynamic forward movement, the Christian uses the words
"the destiny of God." Holiness, transcendence, love, and
destiny—this is the way a Christian describes his experiences of the phenomena of God's spiritual nature.

Israel was always very reluctant to talk about God in
spiritual terms. She felt the need to stress his personal
involvement in human life. This is why the Old Testament
tends to talk about God in human terms. Most religions
that spiritualize God end up with a kind of aloof deism or
a philosophy or pantheism. Israel was determined not to
get lost in byways like that. She recognized the spiritual
nature of God, but she did not belabor it.

It remained for Christianity to synthesize the personal
and spiritual understanding of God, and Christianity did it
in the following way. As the Father of Jesus the Christ,
God is the holy, loving, transcendent one who is moving
toward his destiny; but as the God who was in Christ
reconciling the world to himself he is the one who is
involved and personal and immanent, drawing people into
love. Christianity carefully protected both God's personalness and his spirituality.

Today it is still possible to experience God as Spirit, for
there are times in our lives when the path of the Eternal
Mystery crosses the path of our lives and we stand in the
presence of the phenomenon. We can describe this phe-

nomenon in this way: the completely other, totally pervasive energy of being, relentlessly moving us toward the fulfillment of our unity. That is one way it can be described. But there is another way it can be described: the holy, transcendent God, shaping our lives toward love. I suggest to you that both of these descriptions are ways of talking about the same phenomenon—the phenomenon of the spiritual nature of the covenant God.

## 20. The Covenant God Gives Unity

*Deuteronomy 6:4-9; Isaiah 45:18-25*

The story of Israel's experience of the oneness of God is very important for us as we seek to discover a Christian perspective for the world in which we live. The story goes something like this:

In the early history the Israelites were not monotheists. They had no understanding of the fact that there was just one God. Other gods were recognized as existing and as real; each land and nation and people had its own god, and each god had to be given what was due him. Israel's god happened to have the name Yahweh. But wherever the Israelites went, the gods of that land had to be placated. As Israel began to grow in understanding, however, she began to realize that Yahweh was more than just a god among the gods. The next step was the idea that Yahweh is the king of all the gods. Other gods were still thought to exist, but Yahweh controlled them, and before him they became as nothing. This was a whole new apprehension of truth in the development of human thought. Yahweh was understood as the lord of all lands and peoples and nations and gods. There was an increasing sense of universalism and an increasing intolerance of those who would be rivals of Yahweh. To serve Yahweh alone was the purpose of human existence. It was this insight that gave Israel's leaders their utterly reckless energy and commitment. They joyfully died for him.

As it was gradually realized that Yahweh was not just one among the gods, but that he was king of all the gods,

115

slowly but surely there began to creep into Israel another idea. This idea was that Yahweh perhaps needed a consort. Israel early took her stand against such thinking and said, "There is no consort for Yahweh." There were many attempts to introduce a companion goddess. If Yahweh, after all, could have no rivals he could at least have a friend! That was the very least they could do for their god. But the theology of Israel stood firm against this kind of heresy. Yahweh alone was sufficient within himself, for himself and for man. He asserts and imposes his will with a passionate kind of intensity, and he stimulates men in fear and in gratitude to serve him. He drives them to give themselves to him without fear or thought of the consequences.

Now as this whole idea of a consort for Yahweh became an intolerable idea, a concept that would not be allowed within the covenant community, Israel gradually developed a true monotheism: "Hear, O Israel, the Lord our God, the Lord is one Lord." This was sung from the Temple as the people were called to worship. Here we have another major mutant in the evolution of human religious thought. It develops not out of philosophical speculation, but out of the experience of living with the living God and knowing him as *person* and as *spirit.* They said, "Our experience tells us that Yahweh creates all of life, and there is no part of life he will not determine and control." This was the practical proof of his sole reality.

The last step in Israel's understanding of the oneness of God was a recognition of the power of the world that opposed the will of Yahweh. Late Yahwism (we might better call it early Judaism) developed a very sophisticated demonology. It is important for us to remember that in her demonology the demons were not gods, nor were they rivals of God, but they were powers that were in express opposition to the will of God. We might think that the development of a demonology would be a step backward in a people's religious evolution. In fact, I suggest, this is a very significant and very sophisticated step forward. It is a mythological way of expressing what we all experience in life. Who among us has not experienced real powers that seek to destroy the energy and the power of love? Who among us is not aware that these powers exist in us in opposition to all that would make us godly and human? In fact, these powers are so real that if we fail to name them we have failed to understand the oneness of God. God's destiny is to destroy and overthrow all powers that would stand in opposition to his love. Israel expressed this experience in terms of demons. How shall we express it today—in terms of a word like "anti-love," the forces and the power of anti-love in the world? Find a way to express it—but the expression of the reality of the power that seeks to destroy love is a most important expression if we are to understand God in his oneness.

This is Israel's story of her experience of the oneness of God. We should now ask: How does this story pertain to the story of our own lives? What does that have to do with us today? I would suggest the following. There are levels of human and Christian experience, and the story of Israel's understanding of God is perhaps not a bad way of seeing some of the levels of our own religious perception. We might say that the first level of Christian experience is to live with and try to placate many gods. What would a child list as his gods? Parents? food?—perhaps you can think of others. What would an adolescent list as his gods? His friends? the educational system?—I know many adolescents who stand in real fear of the educational system because—if they do not placate that god, the demons have them forever! How about a man—what would be the gods that he might list? The necessity to produce an income?— many of us know that as a god that holds a ready whip; or our possessions, the things we own? What might a woman list as her gods? An ordered family in which nothing goes askew? social status? Communities of children and adolescents and men and women have their gods, too. What would your community list as its gods? Education? propriety? Perhaps it would not be a bad idea to make a list of your gods. Whom do you worship? What are your priorities? That is what we are really talking about, is it not?

The second level of Christian experience might be a realization that all of these gods are fantasies, that our strength and our salvation (what I would call our humanness) do not lie in them and that they will disappear. With them, if we orient our life toward them, will disappear the orientation of our life. In God alone—in that personal spiritual energy of Love alone—are strength and continuity and meaning for life.

The third level of Christian experience might be an attempt to convert our former gods into friends of God. How hard it is to give up our fantasies! Who really wants to give up something as important as the fantasies by which we live? We beg God: "If I cannot worship them, at least let me tolerate them as innocuous companions to my life—let them still be around me."

A fourth level of Christian experience might be the recognition that God will allow neither friends nor rivals. His reality (this is the hard part of coming to terms with Christianity) means an end to all our fantasies. That is why there are so many churchmen in the world today who are having difficulty being Christian: because it means an end to fantasy. He dominates all of life, giving us power and strength and joy, and all our living is a response to the demands of his will upon us. We are overawed by the realization that God is one and that he has won us. This is the point at which we really begin to understand what it means to love and to be loved.

The last level of Christian experience is a realistic appraisal of the forces around us that would destroy love. These forces will seek to drag us back to the first level or the second or the third. I suggest that this is the pilgrimage or story of faith for any mature believer. A human being may stop at any one of these levels in his Christian experience, and having progressed to any one he may revert to a lower. But I would also suggest that our ability to handle life will be in direct proposition to how much we have experienced the oneness of God. And our joy in life will be in direct proportion to how much we know God as the sole reality whom we worship and serve. The mature and joyous Christian is moving toward an experience of God's sole reality in his existence and is realizing for himself confidence and hope because he serves the will of the only God.

Does the story of Israel's experience and of our own personal experience inform us in any way about the story of the Christian covenant community—the church? It seems to me that the churches indeed try to placate many gods—social order and culture, social status, programs that exist within the church and have become vested interests that no one dares give up, enormous buildings that cannot be afforded, critical members, pietistic religiosity. These are just some of the many gods that the churches worship from time to time.

Then the Christian community—and this is the joy of community—begins to enter into a growing realization that all of these things are fantasies, not gods to be worshipped. We are very privileged people. We are living in one of the rare moments of Christian history. One came in the time of Jesus and Paul, another in the time of Augustine, another in the time of St. Francis, and still another in the time of Luther and Calvin. None has come for a long time now, but in these generations right now we are living in one of those rare moments of Christian history when the churches are discarding all their fantasies. It is a tough time to be living as a Christian. This is why so many church people are disillusioned with the churches, because all their fantasies are being shot down. But for the Christian (not just the churchman, but the Christian) it is a joyous time because he worships and serves beyond fantasy.

The next step may well be a frightened attempt to convert these false gods into the friends of God. We may next begin to hear such things as: "Oh, if the churches could only reform their programs"; "Oh, if the churches could only placate their critical members"; "Oh, if the churches could only find a new form of pietism." It will not work! It would not work with Israel, and it will not work with us. The real joy of the Christian community is finally to realize that the only purpose of the covenant fellowship is to serve and worship the one God. And when we do that in utter joy and in profound privilege, we will come to terms with the fact that there are many forces both inside and outside the churches that are seeking to tear down this service and this worship of God.

But the Christian church will come through. That we can depend on. She will come through on the basis of the experience of the oneness of God. And she will continue to be the people of God. Among those faithful to the covenant, the Holy Spirit will become a moving and gripping power, and the world wants that—it wants a power that is true *power*, not anti-love. The world wants to be loved. The Christian community that knows the power of one God, that worships and serves one God, will be up to loving the world. And it takes a lot of love.

## 21. The Covenant God Gives Power

### Psalm 68:32-35; John 10:17-18

The parent begins with total control over his child. He is God's proxy, and as such he is all-powerful. As the child grows, the mature parent seeks to relinquish this power. He ceases to be the master and seeks to become the partner of the growing child, for he realizes that the exercise of power reaches the point of diminishing returns. To exercise power is to lose control. Thus the mark of the parent's true power is the willingness not to exercise power. If a parent is unwilling to give up the position of power, conflict arises; if, on the other hand, he is willing to do so, maturity results. And as the mature parent exercises his power by refusing to exercise it, three things accrue to the child: first, a deepening sense of his personal responsibility—what we might call a sharpening of his ability to love; second, expanding horizons in interpersonal relationships—what we might call a sense of what it means to live in covenant with other human beings; third, an open future in which the child becomes free to create his own humanity—what we might call hope.

To talk about the power of God in the last half of the twentieth century is difficult. Theologians have peddled a vast array of largely irrelevant material on this score. Most laymen think of the power of God in rather magical terms. Leslie Dewart says that "our frequent insistence on thinking of God as an all-powerful being is not unlike that of the child who insists on thinking of his father as the most muscular and threatening father in the neighborhood." He goes on to say that the problem of the power of God is immaterial to modern man. In order to test that assumption, I asked a number of people, "What is the first thing that comes into your mind when I use the word 'power'?" The responses were interesting. They ranged from one person (a clergymen, by the way), who responded with "Charles Atlas," through the ordinary ones—black power, nuclear power, student power, flower power, United States armaments—to some very sophisticated ones like "the love that binds the family together." I was led to make two conclusions. First, the concept of power is very real among people. There was not a single person that had any trouble responding. Second, the concept of God's power is very unreal. There was not a single person who mentioned it.

For the people of the Old Testament, the people of Israel, the power of God was not unreal. They experienced his power as that spiritual love showered upon them full of personal concern. He released Israel from bondage and made her a light to all the nations of the world. He gave her a covenant as a sign of his power upon her. Now it is true and it must be remembered that Israel often thought of Yahweh her God as the most muscular father on the block. No question about that. She drew near to Yahweh in fear and trembling. She was always aware, however, of his utter loyalty, his utter kindness, and his readiness to help. She always saw Yahweh's power as creative and loving and healing. Thus Israel experienced God's power, living in partnership with a living God.

Today when we think about power we usually think of it in rather negative terms. Power abuses us and limits us. It may even destroy us. Aldous Huxley, writing in an occasional paper for the Center for the Study of Democratic Institutions in 1963, entitled "The Politics of Population," wrote: "Fifty years ago an armed revolution still had some chance of success. In the contest of modern weaponry a popular uprising is foredoomed. Crowds armed with rifles and homemade grenades are no match for tanks. And it is not only to its armament that a modern government owes its overwhelming power. It also possesses the strength of superior knowledge derived from its communication systems, its stores of accumulated data, its batteries of computers, its network of inspection and administration." From Czechoslovakia to Rhodesia to Vietnam to Anguilla that lesson has been well learned. The negative dimensions of power are quite dramatic.

Does power have any positive dimensions? I would suggest to you that it does. I would put it this way: *power demonstrates itself as true power when it is not exercised.* We often hear it said that the United States is the most powerful nation in the world. If that were really true, there would be no need to exercise that power. The acid test of the positive use of power is the ability not to use it.

Can we experience God's power in positive ways? Again I answer yes. We experience it in the following manner. God (or what we might call Love) is and has been exercising power (or what we might call energy) for billions and billions of years. From the very beginning (wherever and whenever and however that was, and we will never know) Love has sought to organize and release love into the creation. This is the ultimate goal (or what we might call destiny) of the evolutionary process: to actualize love.

Now for countless years this goal, this destiny, has been imposed. It has been imposed upon us by God exercising his power. I would like to suggest that we now face a new situation: that for all his shortcomings, for all his sins, for all his wars, for all his evil, *man is still the highest manifestation of love* yet to emerge. What is happening now and has been happening for several hundred years is that man is evolving into his early adolescence. Man is about where a ten- to twelve-year-old child might be. God the Father is no longer anxious to impose his power upon his child, man. In fact, God is ready to relinquish the role of master and enter into partnership with man. As early as Old Testament times God was heard to say, "You have dominion and I will be your partner."

Thus, what God is doing is pushing man into a threefold

maturity. First, there is a deepening sense of our personal responsibility. I suppose we could point to Black Power, as it is being exercised in the world today, as a manifestation of the growth of love. Second, God is pushing us to an expansion of our horizons about interpersonal relations. I suppose that the politics of the international community is a manifestation of the growing understanding of covenant. And third, God is pushing us toward an open future in which we are free to create our own humanity. I would suggest that the urban revolution is a visible manifestation of hope. God no longer allows us to be puppets on the strings of the divine will. He no longer allows us the comfortable magic of omnipotence on which we can fall back. He is pushing us out of the nest and saying: "Fly. For God's sake, fly!"

Do you realize what a fantastic miracle that is? God is not flexing his muscles for us any more. He is saying, "Flex your own muscles, my child." Imagine a God who will push man out of the nest and say, "Fly." That is miracle. The church is recognizing this as miracle, and that is one reason why so many church people are so unhappy with the modern church. They are being told to fly. They do not like that. What is happening is that God is giving up the exercise of his power. He says it is the only way you will become powerful people, mature and responsible people.

This is the meaning of the cross of Jesus the Christ. When Jesus was threatened there in the Garden of Gethsemane, he said, "Don't you think I have the power to call on my Father and he will send seven legions of angels and whatever is necessary to take care of this situation. But I won't do that, and he won't do that. No, we will choose not to exercise power because it is only in this way that you will come to understand responsible maturity" (what we might call salvation). Thus, the cross becomes the sign of God's power, and that means power withheld for the sake of man. The power in that cross is the power that is not exercised. He was killed. Thus Jesus the man enters into mature partnership with God. He assumes all of the responsibility for his own life. He uses his own muscles. He assumes responsibility for the future. There is nothing magic about the life of Jesus. It is just a willingness to accept the freedom to create his own humanity. Jesus accepts and uses the power that God relinquishes to him, and because of this he becomes the Christ. In this way he makes that power available to all people who come after him.

The power of God is exercised in our world not by God, but by men to whom he gives it. In other words, I experience God's power because you are exercising it. That is the gist of what we are trying to get at here. We all experience the power of God because other people are exercising it. Someone is discovering the meaning of life in the midst of debilitating disease—that is the power of God. Christians involved in the ecumenical movement are bringing an end to competition in the mission of the churches— that is the power of God. Somewhere concerned friends are helping someone to face a critical point in life—that is the power of God. Concerned parents are searching for better educational structures—that is the power of God. People are discovering wholeness in life in the face of impending death—that is the power of God. Legislators are demanding an end to hunger—that is the power of God. Scientists are calling for world population ecology—that is the power of God. The concern of the church for those who may face flood disaster—that is the power of God. A gentle word given to calm a troubled life—that is the power of God. Clothes given to charitable organizations for the naked—that is the power of God. A nurse taking just a little bit of extra time on her own time to comfort her patient—that is the power of God. A teenager seeking truth to create his own life—that is the power of God (and any parent who does not recognize it had better learn quickly that it is the power of God). A mother creating a beautiful home—that is the power of God.

You see, there is nothing magic about it. There is no

magic to fall back on. It is we who are the power of God. God has given his power as a sacred trust into our hands, and we experience the power of God because we experience each other exercising it. There is no kingdom coming, Christian, *except we bring it!* In us God places not only his trust but also his hope. He takes the risk. And that is our joy.

## 22. The Covenant God Gives Steadfastness

### Deuteronomy 32:9-14; Mark 11:15-19

Living in a world that is in constant social, economic, political, and cultural change, we begin to wonder if there is anywhere where the ultimate values remain. Constantly we are assaulted by exterior powers that keep our lives in flux, and we wonder: Is there any place where there is a sense of wholeness, of psychological and social and spiritual integration? Is there any norm standing fast against a world that assaults us in so many ways? Is there anything in the world that is steadfast?

The Christian affirmation is yes, there is indeed something that is very steadfast: the concern of God for the needs of men. In a world of turmoil, that stands fast. But God's concern can be looked at in at least two different ways. It might be looked at as a protection. Sigmund Freud in *The Future of an Illusion* talks about it in this way. He sees the protection of God as a protection against uncertainty in nature and in faith, as man's way of creating his own protection against the evils of human society. We think back back to the old hymn "God will take care of you/Through every day/In every way." It is a nice thought. It is also a magical thought, as if there were some kind of fairy dust that could be sprinkled over us, and with it on us we would have nothing at all to be concerned about. This is perhaps the way most Christians think about the steadfastness of their God.

There is, however, another way in which we can look at the concern of God, not so much as a protection, but as a projection—a projection of the human being into mature and responsible personhood. This makes our understanding not magical but ethical. I suggest that this is the Christian perspective on the steadfast love of God.

The content of the life we live together under covenant as Christians is *steadfastness;* the response to being in covenant with each other is to be steadfast to each other. The reason we know about this steadfastness is that we experience it from God. Israel, the covenant community of the Old Testament, experienced the utterly steadfast love of God. His absolutely dependable gifts included justice ("let justice roll down like waters"), freedom ("I have led you out of the land of Egypt, out of the house of bondage"), peace ("I will shatter the spear, and I will break the sword"), obedience ("turn to me and be saved"), and faithfulness ("in me alone is your strength"). Israel took these things and sought to make of them the dependable content of the human life. Justice, freedom, peace, obedience, faithfulness—that is how men are to react to each other. These any man who is living within the covenant will give any other human being.

The problem of course arises when men are not dependable, when they break the steadfastness of their relationship to each other. Instead of justice there is oppression, such as we see exerted against the black man in South Africa or Rhodesia or the United States. Instead of freedom there is bondage, such as we see in Czechoslovakia or Cuba or China. Instead of peace there is war, such as we see in the Middle East or Indochina. Instead of obedience there is rebellion, such as we see in contemporary Israeli nationalism or in anti-ballistic missile systems. Instead of faithfulness there is piousness (and piousness is not faithfulness), such as passes in so many churches today as the content of Christianity.

When men act in these ways of oppression and bondage and war and rebellion and piousness, then all they can expect from God is to be excluded from the divine fellowship. They have relinquished all claim upon the steadfast-

ness of God's holy love. There is only one problem with
this: though men may relinquish their claims upon God,
God does not relinquish his claims upon their lives. In the
face of men's utter undependability God remains dependable. He calls humanity back to justice and freedom and
peace and obedience and faithfulness. Steadfastly he refuses to withdraw his call upon our lives.

Israel understood this; and she provided in her understanding of this a whole new concept in the human understanding of God. Here she probed the depths of the divine
mystery in which God seeks communion with men. This is
not a case of man's searching for God but a case of God's
searching for man. That is a new understanding of God.
Israel said that even though men may try to avoid him and
escape, God will pursue humanity relentlessly. He will give
his call. Francis Thompson, in his poem "The Hound of
Heaven," pictures God as the hound pursuing his prey
until he runs it into the ground and then devours it with
love.

The Hebrews saw in this the great miracle of the covenant God, that the whole creation was full of his steadfastness. There was no escape, no dark corner: "Though I
ascend into heaven, there you will find me. Though I
descend into hell, there you will find me." That is how the
psalmist understood God. And when we read the creed, we
read the words, "He descended into hell." Even in man's
worst hell God will come searching, seeking, calling, asking, pleading, begging, saying to us, "Come back, come
back." This is important because it changes our whole
perspective on life. We cannot get away; yet how many of
us invest enormous amounts of time and energy in running
away from God. We need finally to get straight that it is
impossible. He will hound us to the earth and devour us.
Even when we create hell for ourselves he will devour us
with love.

Does God's steadfastness then mean that things will stay
as they are? Is steadfastness to be equated with the status
quo? If the status quo is composed of oppression and

bondage and war and rebellion and piety, then the answer is obviously no—that is not a part of God's steadfastness. In the Old Testament, from Moses to the prophets, men understood that what God was doing was bringing down the status quo. His ultimate values would overcome all of men's perversions of those values. Psychological and spiritual integration meant turning the society and economy and politics of the system inside out, and God did this time after time after time.

The life of Jesus the Christ is the greatest single testimony to this experience of the really steadfast life. Here in Jesus we meet the psychologically and spiritually integrated person. He stood fast for justice, freedom, peace, obedience, and faithfulness. Because he stood fast he was considered a traitor to the state, an enemy of the people, and a criminal beyond the law. Because he stood fast he was nailed to a cross. Because he stood fast God called him Christ. Tipping over those tables was an act of a totally integrated personality. That was a steadfast person seeking steadfast means and steadfast ends, and we praise that. We say, "Tipping over those tables was a spiritual act of a spiritual man." Let us not fool ourselves. That was a sociological, political, cultural, economic affront to the nation. Because he stood fast, he was nailed fast. Indeed he was a spiritual man doing spiritual things because those are the ultimate things, the things of God, concern for the needs of men. And this is really the central issue—God's concern for the needs of men.

When there is oppression God will steadfastly bring justice. I am an oppressed man. I am oppressed by the military-industrial complex against which the late General Eisenhower warned us. The complex represents a *change* in our society. It owns our industry, our business, our educational system, even our medical schools. Schools created for the most humanitarian of reasons are by and large owned by the military-industrial complex. I am oppressed by that ownership as a human being, and I cry out in my oppression for justice. And I really believe that God will steadfastly turn the military-industrial complex of the United States inside out. And I believe he will do it because he loves us. I believe he will destroy it. He will tip over that table.

When men are in bondage God will steadfastly set them free. The draft is a house of bondage for the young men of our nation. That is a *change;* that is *not* the way it always was. America has never relied in peacetime upon impressed soldiers. It is a negation of everything for which we stand as a great nation, and we are a great nation. This is peacetime. There is no war declared, not even a state of national emergency. Yet we are imprisoning our young men. We are saying to them, "Love your country," while putting them in a system in which they can only hate it. I believe God stands steadfastly against that kind of thing, and I believe that he is going to tip over that table.

Where there is war God will steadfastly bring peace. One of the great virtues of this nation is that we have stood for peace. But there is a *change* in our nation: our government today is preoccupied with war. Martin Luther King said just before he died, "We are the greatest purveyors of death in the world today." Christians, our nation stands for life, not for death, and I believe that God will bring us to our knees for the sins of perpetrating and purveying death. God will tip over that table.

Oh, we praise Jesus for tipping over the tables in the Temple. How do we feel about God's tipping over the tables of our temples today? We have mentioned a few of the life situations in which God steadfastly cares for the needs of men. These are the situations in which he will stand firm, utterly dependable. These are the spiritual and religious issues of our lives because these are the ultimate issues. Justice, freedom, peace, obedience, faithfulness— these are the steadfast things of God, the stable norms in a chaotic world, the ultimate values that stand opposed to anything that will devalue our society. For such stable and ultimate values as these Jesus tipped over the tables of the world, and we praise him and we say, "That is the spiritual act of a spiritual man." His reward was death. They killed him because he tipped over the tables of their world. For such values as these God is steadfastly upsetting the tables of our world, and he will continue to do so. What reward are we preparing for him in our hearts? Will we slay him because in his utter steadfastness he does not agree with us?

Recently I spent a day with my family at the seashore. We were at a lighthouse on the coast. As we sat there above the rocks, the waves came in and crashed against the rocks and sprayed up into the windy sky. As I watched this happening I thought: Look at the chaos of the water banging against the firmness of those rocks that stand there and can never be moved. You know what is wrong with that? It is not the rocks that are stable; it is the water. The water beating against those rocks that day made a few more grains of sand. One day those rocks will be gone.

The rocks are the chaos of the world. They are man's perversion saying: "*We* have built and nothing can destroy *us.*" Our false securities are the rocks. And the waves beat against them and the rocks become sand. In roll the waves of steadfast justice, and sand is created. In roll the waves of steadfast freedom, and more sand is made. In roll the waves of steadfast peace, and our perversions become as sand. In roll the waves of obedience, and the rocks of rebellion are worn away. In roll the waves of faithfulness, and piousness melts. Wave after wave beats against the hardest, most perverse rocks man can throw up against them. The rocks are *new;* they represent *change.* The ocean is unchanging. The ocean is the steadfast will and power of God beating all the rocks we build into sand. He is steadfast all right. Whatever we create that is like a rock, if it is filled with oppression and injustice, with war, with disobedience and rebellion, he will grind into sand, and the waves of justice and freedom, of peace and obedience and faithfulness will prevail.

## 23. The Covenant God Gives Righteousness

### Isaiah 42:5-9; Exodus 22:21—23:9

We hear it said from time to time that if there were no belief in an independently surviving soul to be rewarded or punished in an afterlife, there would be no religious compulsion toward acceptable social behavior. In other words, people who say this are stating that Christian behavior depends on the fear of the survival of the soul. And that is a patently false assumption that totally misinterprets the Christian faith.

The religious compulsion for acceptable social behavior in the Christian faith is not fear for the survival of the soul. The religious compulsion for ethical behavior is based upon two things: first, that my brother exists; second, that I am commanded to love my brothers. My relation to you as my brother has nothing to do with my afterlife. It has to do with the fact that you exist and that I am commanded to love you. This is normative for Christian life.

The righteousness of God—that is what we are talking about. Righteousness means at least two things: first, a willingness to take one's place in the community, and second, a responsible attitude toward the needs of others. Now this attitude of righteousness is demonstrated by and derived from God alone. He is the righteous being. He takes his proper place in the community. You remember what Isaiah wrote: "I have taken you by the hand and I have led you, says the Lord." That is his proper place within the community. He assumes that place; he takes it. He also assumes responsible behavior within the rights and needs of mankind. We read it in the passage in Exodus: "I will hear, for I am compassionate." His compassion, you see, is his responsible attitude toward the rights and the needs of human beings. Such right behavior, we can then say, is predictable in God. He will take his proper place in relation to the community. He will be sensitive to the rights and the needs of mankind, his creation. That is predictable.

But if this compassion is predictable in God, then it should also be predictable in man. It cuts across all of the social, economic, ethical, political, and religious dimensions of life. Recall some of those words from that passage in Exodus: You shall not utter a false report—that is the social dimension. You shall not oppress or wrong any stranger—that is the ethical dimension. You shall not exact interest from a creditor—that is the economic dimension. You shall not pervert justice due the poor—that is the political dimension. You shall be a people consecrated to me—that is the religious dimension. The point is that all of these attitudes provide a full new dimension to human behavior.

What the people of Israel did gives us a whole new insight as to how men ought to behave toward each other. This behavior arises from responsible and sensitive relationships between God and man and between man and man; relationships that eliminate all self-righteousness; relationships that create covenants in which predictable behavior occurs. I can depend on the way you as a Christian will act. You can depend, or ought to be able to depend, on the way I as a Christian will act. There should be a predictableness within our behavior. Such relationships give order and cohesion and stability and security to life; such relationships arise from and give birth to justice.

Understood in this way justice is not an abstract absolute. Justice is an exercise of love that meets a particular contingency. Justice comprises the right and the duty of responsible living. Justice is not an end, but a means—the means of being human with each other. It is a way of safeguarding every person in the community.

This means that righteousness is the act of doing justice. Thus righteousness is a variable constant. It is constant because it must always be done—justice must always be done. But it is variable because each new situation will determine what justice is in that situation, and that may change from situation to situation.

Israel, the covenant people of the Old Testament, understood that Yahweh her God was watching over her to see that she did righteousness. Each person was called to take his place in the community. He could not be self-righteous. He could not step outside the community and say, "I will determine whether I will take my place or not." And the community was to exercise responsible attitudes toward the needs of others. The community was not at liberty to say, "Yes, this man in his need deserves my help, but that man in his need does not deserve my help." Human beings deserve help.

One of the tragedies in the contemporary churches is the loss of the sense that God is watching over us to see that we do justice. Think about that for a moment. How many of us really have a powerful motivating sense that God is watching over us *to see* that we do justice? Perhaps the failure of Christians to be sensitive to this kind of pressure is what has allowed the churches so often to slip into what we might call self-righteousness. Israel affirmed that God established his righteousness in the hearts of his people. This inner renewal of the heart changed the character of the person and of the whole community. It was an inner renewal of the individual and a just ordering of society; and these two put together, in the Old Testament conception, were called the salvation of God. God's intent was to help every human being discover the dimensions of salvation. Therefore, God hears the cry of the oppressed and the suffering and the sinning.

Every cry of every sinful man is heard by our God. This

eliminates all abstract ideas about correct behavior. Righteousness is not a philosophy. Righteousness is a way of life manifested in concrete relationships between people. Justice means mending broken lives and mending broken societies. That is what we are called to be about as Christians. To do justice is to reconcile, to love each other, every man, every oppressed and suffering and sinning man. The only way, then, that we as Christians can glorify God is to dedicate ourselves to each other's needs.

The paramount manifestation of this whole process was, of course, Jesus of Nazareth. In him we discover the totally righteous human life. He took his place in the community. He was sensitive to the needs of others. He demonstrated the ultimate dimensions of human behavior. Through Jesus, whom we call the Christ, man was freed to be righteous. We were set free to be righteous people. And the implications of being righteous become clear, both its dangers—the cross—and its hopes—the resurrection. You see, what God graciously gives to man is the gift of being responsible for his own destiny. What Christ was to man each man now becomes to every other man: the righteous one. This is God's great risk and mankind's great opportunity.

Can we identify any practical applications of this kind of righteousness? I would suggest, to take one example, that righteousness is the expansion of the food stamp program. I believe that every human being has a right to eat and that any society which calls itself just has an obligation to see that every person in that society eats. I do not think it is the responsibility of man to forage for his food. We do not even make domesticated animals do that. It therefore becomes the obligation, as I understand it, of every society to feed the people in that society. Thus I see the expansion of the food stamp program as a sensitive response to the rights and the needs of human beings. This is a society doing justice, being righteous. It encourages people to take their place in the society.

There is no dearth of issues in contemporary society

that will test our ability to exercise righteous behavior. The entire area of race relations is a familiar issue that is testing our righteousness in America today. There are people on all sides of that issue who are being very self-righteous. There are others who are trying desperately to do justice. On such issues as these we are being tested with regard to our Christian moral behavior. Are we taking our place within the community? Are we being responsible to the rights and the needs of our fellow men? Are we doing justice? Are we being righteous?

To live out God's righteousness we have no choice but to be in a responsible attitude toward the needs of others. Anything less than doing what he intends us to do is unrighteousness. And the joy of what we have is our opportunity as human beings to do what God intends us to do. That is it, that is righteousness—to do what God intends us to do.

## 24. The Covenant God Gives Love

*Hosea 2:16-20*

It is a beautiful, sensitive, tender story about a man and a woman that our Scripture passage relates. The man had been called to be a minister. He had started his career and was faithful as God's preacher. Then one day he met a charming and beautiful woman, and fell in love with her. It was the kind of love that we all yearn for at some time in our lives—full of tenderness, concern, compassion, care. He asked her to be his wife. But there was a serious problem. Before she met the preacher, she had lost her virginity. Despite this the man and the woman were married. He was sure in his strength that for all the bad reputation that hovered round her, he would renew her, and that in his arms she would become pure and faithful.

For some time the two lived together in bliss and happiness. They had three beautiful, strong, sturdy children. But living with a preacher is not the easiest thing in the world. Soon the wife returned to her old ways and was unfaithful to her husband. So blatantly unfaithful was she that he would no longer live with her. Finally he reached that critical breaking point, where he said, "This cannot go on. I shall have to divorce you." And so he did. The pain and the torment within his own soul were so great that he even changed the names of the children so that all memory of his dear and beloved wife would be wiped from his remembrance.

There was only one problem—his love for this woman would not go away. Day after day he ate his heart out in

138

the compulsive and profound love he still felt for her. Finally when he could tolerate it no longer, he went and searched for her; but could not find her. His quest went on and on through all the places where he thought she might be, and in his sorrow as he searched, he wept. While walking through the slave market in utter dejection one day, he saw her being auctioned as a slave. In utter joy he bought his wife back, and returned home with her. He remarried her, changed the names of the children back, and their life together was reestablished.

A beautiful, tender, gentle story, a story that stands in the Old Testament as the greatest single testimony to the meaning of the love of God. The compulsion that drove Hosea to love Gomer is the compulsion that drives God to love his children. God created the world, and out of his creation he chose a people to be a light to this world. It was a people of very bad reputation. They were in slavery in Egypt, but he said, "I will love you." So he bought them out of slavery, and he married that people. He made a covenant with his new bride Israel. That people was unfaithful, utterly, totally unfaithful, deserving nothing but the worst punishment, deserving utter divorce from her God. But God searched for that people and loved that people and brought that people back and said, "I will not abandon you. I will love you." For Israel, the story of Hosea and Gomer became the living demonstration of what it means to say that God is love.

In the Old Testament there are three major overtones that express divine love. First is the complete engagement of the will, like the love of a husband for his wife and a wife for her husband. Second is compassion for the helpless, like a mother's love for her child. Third is concern for the needs of others, such as the love of a rich man for a poor man. Hosea's experience expressed all of these dimensions of love in a most profound way. God's love is consuming, irrational love: as consuming as the love of a mother for her child or a wife for her husband, as irrational as the love of a rich man for his poor brother. But

Israel was totally unfaithful to this love, and this was the root of her alienation from God. She deserved nothing but total punishment. In this situation the amazing miracle is that God condescends to the hapless people. Instead of punishing them he loves them more!

In the play "A Raisin in the Sun," Mama says this:

> "There is always something left to love. If you ain't learned that, you ain't learned nothing. Have you cried for that boy today? I don't mean for yourself and for the family 'cause we lost money. I mean for him. Have you cried for him, what he has been through and what it has done to him? Child, when do you think is the time to love somebody the most—when they done good and made things easy for everybody? Well, then you ain't through learning because that ain't the time to love at all. It's when he's at his lowest and can't believe in himself 'cause the world done whipped him so. When you starts measuring somebody, measure him right, child. Measure him right. Make sure you done take into account all the hills and the valleys he come through before he got where he is now."

*Make sure you done take into account all the hills and the valleys he come through before he got where he is now.* That is God. That is the love of God. He takes into account all our hills and valleys and he loves us! That is the kind of love that transcends all human thought patterns.

God seeks to touch the tender heart in man, and this is the basis of the covenant relationship, the relationship of brotherly love and godly love. This relationship replaces law with the fellowship of love. Man becomes the object of divine love, and in this position total allegiance is demanded. Man's response to the divine love is to live in a loving way. God's love cannot be reduced to a moral principle. God's love flies in the face of all legalism and all morality. If Hosea had done what was socially right—what was acceptable—he would have had nothing more to do with Gomer. If God had done what was religiously right, he would have had nothing more to do with Israel. If God were to do what was "right," he would have nothing more to do with you or me. We do not deserve his love. We only get it. God sets us free in his love by capturing us with more love.

But then we suddenly discover ourselves to be in a perilous situation. You see, God will not allow that kind of love to be perverted or broken. Man's way of life must be God's way of love. The danger is that a love that demands all of this cannot but destroy everything that resists it. If we pervert that love or break it or stand in its way, God's response is still to love us until we are brought to our knees. This is a dread that should cause us to shudder in the innermost parts of our being.

This is a love that presses forward toward a new world order. Justice must be done in the inner heart of man and in the social order. The most sublime manifestation of that suffering (that dimension of love) is, of course, Jesus of Nazareth. He assimilated into himself all of the burdens of the oppressed and the suffering and the afflicted and the sinning. Can you imagine (no, we cannot imagine because it does not mean anything to us any more)—he held the hand of a leper! One just did not do that, *but he did.* Can you imagine being willing to die rather than not do justice? Can you imagine the kind of love that reestablishes the covenant, the kind of love that re-creates the fellowship, the kind of love that remarries all of us who have broken our promises?

Such love as this must be preserved to the very end. God will not and man dare not let it evaporate from this creation. This is the crux of what I want to say in this sermon: only in the presence of the fellowship of love is there any hope for the world. Take love away from this world (or just allow it to evaporate), and all of human life becomes futile and abysmal. If this world is to continue and if the human race is going to continue, there must be a demonstration of what it means to love. There must be people who are saying to the world, "I am loved." There must be people who are saying to the world, "I love you." Without that this world is dead.

Now the task of the church, the task of the Christian

fellowship, the task of people of covenant is to demonstrate that kind of love to the world. The world is our Gomer and we its Hosea, because we are God's Gomer and he has been our Hosea. This is the only reason the church exists—to love the world.

We wonder how this applies to us, specifically to us, our little selves. It is only when we finally recognize that we are the Gomers of the world and God is our Hosea that all of it becomes meaningful. God has married us, and we have been unfaithful, but he has loved us even in our unfaithfulness. Our task, not just as a church, but as persons living within that church, is to show that to the world.

In my experience I think I have finally learned that really the only thing people are seeking in this world is to be loved. That is all. People come to me distraught and confused, and I am learning that the thing they want most is to hear someone say to them, "I love you. Yes, you have done all those stupid things. Yes, all that has happened to you. Yes, I accept all that. But I love you, and nothing you will ever do will take away that love." The world needs to learn finally to say to each other: "I accept you for what you are. I understand your problems and I love you." Teilhard de Chardin says it this way: "Some day after mastering the winds and the waves and the tides and gravity, then we shall harness for God love—and then for a second time in the history of the world man will discover fire."

The world needs fire. Your love is fire. God's love for you is fire. Let it burn and be yourself consumed. And then consume the world.

## 25. The Covenant God Gives Wrath

*Hosea 3*

If you had to list those people whose actions call for retribution and judgment, whom would you mention? The drug addict—certainly the laws of the state say that he demands judgment. The alcoholic, the adulterer—these are people who often tear the fabric of the family apart. The arsonist—whom, it is suggested, we should "shoot to kill." The looter—whom, it is suggested, we should shoot to maim. The assassin—we execute. The anarchist—sometimes we jail. The policeman—sometimes we brutally malign him. The military deserter—we send him into exile. The income tax cheater—he is fined.

But in such a list would you include the wife who treats her husband as a thing instead of a person? The father who treats his children as things instead of persons? The boss who treats his secretary as a thing instead of a person? The Christian, allowed to keep 90% of what he has received from God, who refuses to return 10%? These are very simple things, but are not these the kinds of situations where judgment is deserved? In all these kinds of situations we have named, the fragile fabric of human relationships is destroyed, and the wrath of God becomes operative.

The Bible uses some striking imagery for those people who dehumanize themselves and other people. They are said to go into a "far country." Or they are said to be "dead": such persons have ceased to exist as human beings.

Our human instinct is to punish those people who step

143

beyond the limits of our defined order. We seem rather sure that we know how to equate the exercise of the anger of men with the wrath of God. I was talking recently with a wonderful and venerable friend of mine, and he said something that struck me: "I am deeply concerned about the punitive mood of my contemporaries. They seem to know just who should be punished and how to punish them." Another illustration of how this occurs is what is happening to clergymen in the world today. There are many people who feel that the clergy of the contemporary church are in a "far country," because we put concern for people ahead of concern for property or even principles. I think that is true. Among the clergy in the churches (and among many Christians in the churches) there is today a deep concern for people, ahead of either property or principles. And there is quite an impressive amount of energy from churchmen directed toward punishing clergy for that position. Funds are withheld. Accusing and derogatory comments are often made. People withdraw their participation from the church. This is often an attempt to punish the clergy, but it really, unfortunately, punishes only the church of Jesus Christ. If such people only realized that there are more effective means of being creative Christians than that.

It is quite astonishing how eager many people are to exercise wrath. It is incredible how certain we can be as to who should be punished and how to punish them. The wrath of God is something man is quite eager to get his hands on, rather like fire in Greek mythology. If we could finally presume that the anger of man could be equated with the wrath of God, then, you see, we could have complete self-justification. I cannot help wondering what the result would be if we were as eager to exercise the love of God as we are to exercise the wrath of God.

There was a radical dimension to the understanding of God's wrath among the people of the Old Testament. They said that wrath—unlike grace—was never a permanent attribute of God. Wrath comes when one person destroys the personhood of another person. But more important, wrath goes when one person exalts the personhood of another. The individual under God's wrath is out of relation with his brothers. You can identify such persons by their outlook on life, by their attitude toward the world and their brothers, by their temper. Think of the people you know. You can identify people who are under the wrath of God because they are not being human to their brothers, can you not? You can identify them by their temper, their outlook on life, the attitude of unease within their own life.

The important thing is that the wrath of God is not understood as reward or punishment. The wrath of God is the fearsome tension that demands that every man love his brother no matter what that brother has done. That is the exercise of the wrath of God. I like to think of wrath and grace as the two hands of God's love. When we are unloving toward our brothers, God reaches out and lays his hand on us. He takes us by the collar, shakes us, and says, "I demand that you return to your human capabilities." That is the wrath of God, loving us back into our humanity. When we are obedient to our humanness, then the hand of God comes out to us, and he lays it upon our shoulder and loves us—those are the two hands of God's love. I would suggest to you that this is the situation to which we must very humbly and very gratefully resign ourselves: that for good or for ill, in wrath and in grace, God loves us. No man, no matter what he has done, can get away from that. God loves him.

Jesus took this Old Testament viewpoint and honed it to its finest precision. Let me read you Jesus' comment on the wrath of God. Jesus said:

> "There was a man who had two sons; and the younger of them said to his father, 'Father, give me the share of the property that falls to me.' And he divided his living between them. Not many days later, the younger son gathered all he had and took his journey into a *far country*, and there he squandered his property in loose living. And when he had spent everything, a

great famine arose in that country, and he began to be in want.
So he went and joined himself to one of the citizens of that
country, who sent him into his fields to feed the swine. And
he would gladly have fed on the pods that the swine ate; and
no one gave him anything. But when he came to himself he
said, 'How many of my father's hired servants have bread
enough and to spare, but I perish here with hunger! I will arise
and go to my father, and I will say to him, "Father, I have
sinned against heaven and before you; I am no longer worthy
to be called your son; treat me as one of your hired servants."'
And he arose and came to his father. But while he was yet at a
distance, his father saw him and had compassion, and ran and
embraced him and kissed him. And the son said to him,
'Father, I have sinned against heaven and before you; I am no
longer worthy to be called your son.' But the father said to his
servants, 'Bring quickly the best robe, and put it on him; and
put a ring on his hand, and shoes on his feet; and bring the
fatted calf and kill it, and let us eat and make merry; for this
my son was dead, and is alive again; he was lost, and is found.'
And they began to make merry."

That is a parable about the wrath of God. That is the
Christian exposition of what it means to be living under
God's wrath. The son had gone into a far country. But
what is his father's response? Compassion, an embrace, a
kiss. How many of you would not do that for your child?

You see, God exercises his wrath by receiving his wayward children back in joy. How many of us are not
wayward? How many of us do not need to be received
back that way? If there is any one who is so perfect and so
pure that he can say to God, "I don't need to be received
back by you," that man does not have any need of the
church. Here is a whole new dimension of our human
behavior. This is how we are to exercise the wrath of God.

But, someone may argue, doesn't this view ignore the
fact that the son had to return. The father did not go off
after him to bring him back. The son had to make a
decision and he had to come back. Let me read you
something else. This is our Lord again:

"What man of you, having a hundred sheep, if he has lost one
of them, does not leave the ninety-nine in the wilderness, and

go after the one which is lost, until he finds it? And when he has found it, he lays it on his shoulders, rejoicing. And when he comes home, he calls together his friends and his neighbors, saying to them, 'Rejoice with me, for I have found my sheep which was lost.' Just so, I tell you, there will be more joy in heaven over one sinner who repents than over ninety-nine righteous persons who need no repentance."

This is how the Christian exercises wrath on his fellow men. He discerns when they are in a far country, when they are dead. He goes there and he searches them out. He brings them back and he welcomes them in compassion, with an embrace and a kiss, and he rejoices and says, "I love you, and so does God." It is the task of the church and of every individual Christian to exercise the wrath of God. Now perhaps we should go back to the list we made at the beginning of this sermon and ponder what it would mean to exercise the wrath of God on each of the people we had on our list.

But, you say, that is unrealistic for the world in which we live. That is impractical. I think that is true. It *is* totally and completely unrealistic in terms of the world in which we live. But I think it is equally true that the church is not called to live under the realism dictated by the world. That is why we are Christians. That is why we call ourselves by a name that separates us from all the rest of the world. The church is not called to accept the standards of the world, but to change them. We may not like the understanding of the exercise of wrath in this way. It may go against everything that is ingrained within us. It does in me. But that is quite unimportant, because that is the Christian stance. The Christian (not necessarily just the *churchman*, but the *Christian*), even though he may not like it, will be obedient to it, because that is the gospel he has. The non-Christian may not be obedient to it and he may not like it, but that is quite irrelevant. That is why he is a non-Christian (even though he may be a churchman).

Many Christians become uncomfortable when they are attacked at this point by their non-Christian friends, who

say, "You don't stand for things like that, do you?" The
Christian response is "Yes, that is what I stand for." And
then he rejoices in his own security because he realizes that
it is not really himself who is uncomfortable or else they
would not need to attack his position. You see, the world
knows that the unrealism of Christianity is more hopeful,
and the world does not want to have to deal with that kind
of hope.

So the Christian rejoices, because as a Christian he is set
free to love and embrace his wayward brothers. He has no
obligation to punish anyone, only to love them. And that
is why the Christian can relax during crises that put other
people uptight, because the Christian's only obligation is
to love people. As a Christian that is all you are called
upon to do, to rejoice and love your wayward brothers—
and then you will be exercising the wrath of God.

## 26. The Covenant God Gives Holiness

*Isaiah 6:1-9*

It is both humbling and exalting to realize that the essence of the divine is contained in the being of the human. This is the Christian affirmation: man is created to be the temple of God's Spirit. To put that in contemporary terms, we might say that man's destiny is to actualize the purposes of God's love.

These temples of the Lord and his Spirit come in all sizes and shapes and personalities. Some are thin and some are fat; some are tall and some are short; some are wise and there are some that are not so wise. There are a myriad of exteriors, but it is the inside that makes the difference. For it is on the interior that life is beautiful or ugly, sweet or sour, noble or base. The task of each man and of all mankind is to discover the dimensions of dignity and destiny that bind each man all the more closely to God, who holds both human dignity and human destiny in his Eternal Mystery. Mankind and each man is the recipient and vessel of God's holiness.

Old Testament religion was the first to explore this dimension of human existence. Holiness has many facets, and we cannot discuss them all in this sermon, but the one we shall talk about is this: holiness is that mystery which is at the most profound depths of our being human. The earliest understandings of holiness said that God was totally removed from men. The Old Testament people brought a new insight to this. They said that God's purpose in loving men is to make mankind more personal and more holy. Another way of saying this is that God wants every one of us to share in the profound mystery of being. Whenever a man encounters the divine he is over-whelmed by the impact. We stand on the brink of the ultimate abyss. We are at once repelled in terror (we cannot stand to be accosted by the divine in that way) and attracted in awe, for we know that if we do not receive what it will offer there is no hope for our lives. We are being threatened by the mystery at the root of our being—standing in the presence of something that is totally other than ourselves and calling us to be more than we are.

This is why Isaiah was overwhelmed and undone and lost. He was standing on the brink of the ultimate abyss. His whole being was being called into question, and out of that experience he became the recipient of God's holiness. God gave the Eternal Mystery into the care of Isaiah.

I suggest to you that this is the key to the understanding of man's destiny, to the understanding of our own per-sonal destiny. We are called to bear the mystery of being human. In religious terms, our task is to be temples of God's holiness. In contemporary, secular terms, our task is to bear the mystery of being human. In this way each human being is facing a decision that strikes at the root of his own being. Every one of us is being called to accept or reject the reason for which we have been given life. We must say "yes" or "no" to the mystery of our being, and there is no middle ground. We must affirm or deny the capacities of our humanity. Our whole existence is at stake in the response we give to God's holiness.

The person who affirms life does justice, mercy, and love to his brother. That is the criterion. Man's participa-tion in God's mystery is confirmed by his ethics. John, in one of his letters, writes, "The man who loves God and hates his brother is not a human being."

The claim that Christians make is that Jesus of Nazareth is the supreme affirmation, the definitive "yes" to life. His whole being was a search for justice and mercy and love. He explored the furthest reaches and depths of the mysteries of human existence. He became the totally human being. For that reason Christians call him the Christ—not because he was some peculiar, extraterrestrial kind of being shot into the world from outer space, but because he was the fully human being. His whole life was a holy life. Everything that he contacts becomes holy. His being defines the dimensions, the potential reaches of our own existence. He was what we are expected to be.

St. Paul puts this in sharp relief when he says, "You are God's temple, and God's mystery dwells in you." Think about that: *God's mystery dwells in you.* God has poured his being into our being. What does that mean? It means that we are required to live up to the ultimate expectations of our humanness. Not that we are required to be religious fanatics or some strange kind of creatures, but that we are required to live up to the ultimate dimensions of our humanness—to do justice, to act out mercy, to give love. Many people imagine that they can enjoy their creation by God, that they can just go around and sop up the world he gives them like some sort of sponge, that they can snap their fingers and expect his protection, that they can engage in some kind of pietistic rituals at their convenience, and he will naturally engage in communion with them. Many people go about with that kind of notion, never bothering about the fundamental expectations God has for us. I was talking with a person the other day who made this statement, "I just don't see what you get all riled up about the Negro problem for. It doesn't have anything to do with religion. I am a religious person; I talk to God every day and I don't pay any attention to the Negro problem." I suggest to you that that is the purest form of utter nonsense. That is heresy at its grossest. Such a person as that has missed the whole point of being human. The man who says he loves God and hates his brother is not a human being.

Peter expands upon Paul's theme and develops it into a definition of the church: "The church is a holy nation called to declare the wonderful mystery of being of a God who called us out of the darkness of our inhumanity into the marvelous light of our humanness." Some people ask: Why does the church exist at all? What is it for? To do justice, to act out mercy, to give love—that is it. To give a continuous "yes" to the capacities of being human. To hold mankind at the brink of the ultimate abyss of the mystery of life. To demand a response from every single human being about the potential of his existence. To demand from every one of us the "yes" or "no" to life. Whether you are in the church or not in the church, the church is saying to you, "Are you affirming or denying the capacities of your humanity? Are you giving a 'yes' or a 'no' to the life that you have been given?" Whether you are a Christian or not, you are being called to decision. "Who will go for me?" "Lord, send me." That is the man who knows his humanness. And to him God says, "Go!"

## 27. The Gifts of the Covenant God

*Genesis 1:26-31; Psalm 145*

What are you thankful for? What does God give you for which you are most devoutly and profoundly thankful? This is a day to be thankful. Every time Christians worship together it is a day, a time, a moment of thanksgiving. That is why we call it a celebration. We come together to tell the story of the faith; but also, and most importantly, to give thanks for those good gifts which God has given into our hands. The scripture from Genesis tells us that the dominion of God is placed in the hands of men. Do you realize that all of what God is, is laid in your hands, and you are told to exercise his authority? That is the story Christians tell. That is the gift for which we give thanks.

In the nine sermons preceding this one we have been talking about the attributes or qualities of the covenant God, what it is that makes him unique and special. But there has been one central theme running through all of that: everything which makes God what God is, is a gift which he gives his children. Just as any father who creates an inheritance for his sons or daughters gives it to his children, so God gives his gifts into the hands of his children. What I have tried to do in those sermons is to readjust our thinking about what these gifts of God are.

When we think of the gifts of God, we often think of the flowers and the trees, the sky and the earth, our families and friends—and all those are gifts of God. But precious as those are, they are not the most important gifts of our Father. What are the gifts of God that Christians celebrate?

First, our own unique personhood. There is not another person like you in the world: billions of people have lived throughout history, and there has never been another one like you, nor will there ever be. You have unique personhood as a gift of your Father.

Second, the spirit within you: a spirit that is created and molded and shaped so that your inner life blooms and becomes beautiful, something that others can look at and say, "There is something different about that person."

The third gift of God to you is a bringing together into one whole of all the scattering of your life and the diversity of your days. He brings it down to one central part of your being, so that you may be a bulwark for other people and you may give forth to the world the love of God.

Then God gives you his power. He does not exercise it himself. He gives it into your care and he says: "Take it and fill this world with justice and mercy and peace. You have dominion; I give my power to you."

When you exercise this power, you exercise some of his other gifts. His steadfastness—he is dependable—the steadfastness which enables you to be dependable for other men. Because you join covenant with him and with each other, your brothers can depend on you. When their lives are distraught and scattered and broken, you give them strength. And you exercise his righteousness—the righteousness that allows you to take your place in the community of believers and the community of all men; the righteousness that calls you to minister in compassion to the needs of those who are nearest to you. And you exercise the gift of love—a love that holds you strongly and tenderly in its care, but also drives you forward and outward, so that you may say to the people around you, "I love you and all I ask from you is to be loved." Those are the gifts of power.

God gives you his wrath, the wrath that we spoke of

earlier as the "other hand" of his love. It is wrath that brings forgiveness and reconciliation. It is not the anger of men: there is a very clear difference between the exercise of the anger of men and the wrath of God. The wrath of God is forgiving and compassionate and reconciling, never hurtful and destructive and demonic. The exercise of reconciliation and forgiveness and compassion—that is the exercise of the wrath of God.

Finally, the last gift that we talked about was the gift of holiness, poured out upon us, freely given to us, calling us to be holy temples of the Spirit of the Lord; to take up our own humanity and to exercise it by being human to other beings.

Personhood, spirit, unity, power, steadfastness, righteousness, love, wrath, holiness—these are not the things we commonly consider when we talk about the gifts of God. And yet these are the most profoundly important gifts that God gives us for our dominion over his world. Without them we are nothing. With them we exercise all that God intends his world to be. So come and celebrate, come and give thanks, but let us be very sure of what we give thanks for. Yes, the trees, the sky, the beautiful day—but not most profoundly. Down in the furthest recesses of our being, we give thanks for those gifts that God gives into our hands which are his very being. Rejoice, celebrate, give thanks for a God who gives himself to you.

## 28. Sealing the Covenant with God

### I Kings 19:9-19

Recently I saw a news clip on television reporting the election of a new mayor in one of our large cities. After he had received the congratulations of his opponent, he went to the microphone and said, "The first thing I am going to do as mayor is to make my first appointment to my council. I want you to know that to the council of this city I hereby appoint *God.*" Strange, isn't it, this mail-order god we seek? When we need him we write out the order and send it in, and we expect that our order will come back packaged the way we wanted it. We see the same kind of thing in the Dial-a-Prayer craze. If we get uptight, we can dial a certain number, and there is instant inspiration. All we need to do is listen to it and be soothed by the spiritual salve.

The people of the Old Testament could never have comprehended that kind of god. They would not have understood what we are talking about when we respond to life in ways like this. For them God dumps into life the enormous and dangerous potential of his being. He takes all those wonderful gifts that he would give us—which we have talked about for many sermons—the gifts of person-hood, of the inner spirit of God, of his steadfastness and his power, of love, of wrath, of holiness—he takes all of those gifts and pours them into our lives. Through them he directly confronts each one of us with his Eternal Being. This is not a god that can be manipulated or managed or appointed to the city council. Man cannot conjure God. God can only give to man.

The gifts of God bring man to the brink of an ultimate decision. Each one of us must choose to accept or to refuse those gifts. Each one of us must choose to be obedient or disobedient to the being that God gives us. And here is the really critical issue: obedience. That has become an unacceptable word in our culture. I remember having a somewhat heated altercation with a friend of mine over the understanding of Christian obedience, and he was making the point that he was not about to obey anybody, even God. Yet when he was in the Army, this person had obeyed without question the commands of his First Sergeant. He never questioned that, but now he was quite willing to state that he was not about to obey anybody, not even God. Perhaps we resist because the inner qualities for obedience—the inner listening to the voice of the Lord—do not exist within us; and we are not quite sure what we ought to obey. Yet this is the question that the church holds up to each person: Are you manipulating God for your own devices or are you obeying God for the sake of his Kingdom?

Now for the man who makes the choice of obedience, there is no rest. There is no opportunity to entrench and set up a secure position. This is what Elijah tried to do and he found out it would not work. There can only be a continual reaching out to grasp the gifts of the Eternal Mystery. The Christian is a man who is spurred on to the greater dimensions of life. He is the man who is willing to take his position on the perilous frontier of justice and love and mercy. In doing this the Christian holds in tension the chaos of the present world and the emerging hope of God's destiny. And that is no mean trick, because that means living inside the Kingdom of God. It is out of this tension, out of holding together the chaos of the world and the emerging hope of God's destiny, that there emerges what knowledge of God we ever have in our lives.

This knowledge of God is not a system of thought; it is

a living experience of the mystery at the very depths of our being. Out of this experience of God with us, norms of conduct and action are developed. These must constantly be reviewed and revised as our knowledge of God grows and develops. And this is why the obedient man can never relax. Life is a constant discovery of God, an unceasing search for the responsible ethical norm, an unrelenting grasping after the meaning of life. What the obedient man does is to realize that the grace of God is directed relentlessly at him. He simply cannot avoid or escape the gifts of God that are laid upon him. This is what we understand as the election of God.

We are elected to be loved by God. God educates us to this election by demanding that we love our brothers. We learn to love God by practicing on each other. That is what you are here for, to allow somebody to practice loving you. That is not easy, but it is the way of the knowledge of God. This is the experience of the divine in our lives. This educative loving extends to every human being. We are not as Christians excused from loving any man.

The practice of Christian love is not selective; it is universal. This means that a radical student fulfills his humanness only when he can love a policeman. That does not include calling a policeman a pig, or calling any other human being a pig. On the other hand, it also means that the conservative alumnus fulfills his humanness only when he can truly love the bearded, long-haired, sandaled radical.

The miracle is God's insistence on being involved in our mixed-up lives. This shatters all our conceptions of retribution, for by our standards it is totally unreasonable that God should care for us. Yet he does.

So what is our response to these gifts and this care of God? The obedient man can only respond humbly in utter gratitude. In Old Testament language this is "sealing the covenant." In the words of Sören Kierkegaard this is taking the "leap of faith."

Jesus lived out of that context. His whole life was an

obedient response of gratitude to the gifts of God. He never had time to rest or relax in his search for the knowledge of God. It led him down dangerous new paths of conduct and action, but he accepted the election of love that God laid upon him. By the standards of men he deserved a reward. He got one. We call it the crucifixion. By the standards of God he deserved vindication. We call that the resurrection. That is why he is the Christ. It takes great courage to follow that kind of line.

Paul was made of that kind of stuff too. "One thing I do," he said, "forgetting what lies behind and straining forward to what lies ahead, I press on toward the goal for the prize of the upward call of God in Jesus Christ." In our generation Teilhard de Chardin is a man made of that kind of stuff. Denounced by his church, exiled from his homeland, persecuted for his beliefs, for seventy years Teilhard never ceased and never rested and never relaxed. Every day he sought to live with the experience of God in the depths of his being. And he gave the world probably its greatest vision of the Christian life since St. Francis.

What does all this mean for our lives? What does this have to say to our times? What is the word of God for me now? It seems to me these things. First, it is time for all of us to give up all our attempts to manage and manipulate God. We will all have to pause and consider very carefully how we shall do this, because it will be exceedingly hard. We have become very skilled at managing and manipulating our fabricated god according to our standards. But we must realize that the religious fortifications that we have built so well are utterly worthless. Second, it is time to choose to live with the constant experience of God in the inner depths of our being. That is the only way we will know what obedience means. The knowledge of God comes by living with God deep inside ourselves, and that is a perilous task. The Kingdom of God comes by practicing love on our brothers, and that is a risk. Yet we must realize that it is only as we face this peril and this risk that we become human, and this will allow us no time to relax in our search. And finally, it is time to revise all our norms of conduct so that they coincide with God's election rather than our desire. Justice and love and peace allow no man time for rest. If we drop our guard for a moment oppression and hate and war will engulf us. The test of obedience is the constancy of our love.

You see, life is a continuous experiment, an unceasing discovery. That is the source of its overwhelming joy and its eternal hope, because the person who will finally resign himself to this fact will have the peace of God that passes all of man's best understanding. The devout and faithful Christian will obey the call of God to this kind of life in joyous gratitude. To search and to risk and to know the peril—that is gratitude! And it was this kind of gratitude that created whole new dimensions of life for Elijah and Jesus and Paul and St. Francis and Teilhard. This kind of gratitude—a gratitude without rest and relaxation, a gratitude of constancy—can create new life and new joy and new hope for us. The only question is: How grateful do we dare to be?

# A Litany for Covenant Life

*Liturgist:* We give thanks to you, O God,
  we give joyous thanks;
  We call upon your name,
  and recount your wondrous gifts:
*People:* For the gift of our unique personal being: Lord,
  nourish in our personal lives such beauty that we may
  become your language of love to those we meet day by
  day.
*Liturgist:* You have made us little less than yourself,
  and crowned us with glory and honor;
  You have given us dominion over the work of
  your hands!
*People:* For the gift of spirit: Lord, create, shape, mold
  our inner lives so that we may be instruments of harmony and serenity drawing those about us into a circle
  of understanding and peace.
*Liturgist:* The Spirit of God has given us life;
  it is upon us for refreshment, strength,
  and aid.
*People:* For the gift of unity: Lord, draw our scattered
  living down into a single center of purpose and intent,
  upon which other people may learn to depend and rely
  for strength and comfort.
*Liturgist:* Behold, how good and pleasant it is when
  brothers dwell in unity!
  For the Lord has commanded this blessing.
*People:* For the gift of power: Lord, inspire us to exercise

it so that the lives of those most dear to us may be filled with justice, mercy, and love overflowing from us.

*Liturgist:* He gives power to the faint,
    and to him who has no might he increases
        strength.

*People:* For the gift of steadfastness: Lord, supply us with such firmness that we may be an anchor of sturdiness for those whose lives are buffeted and battered by the changes and trials of life.

*Liturgist:* For the steadfast love of God is from everlasting to everlasting upon those who fear him.

*People:* For the gift of righteousness: Lord, give us the insight to take our responsible place in the community of men and minister with compassion to the deepest needs of those nearest to us.

*Liturgist:* He calls to the heavens and to the earth:
        "Gather to me the righteous ones who made
        covenant with me."
    The heavens declare his righteousness,
        for God himself is righteous.

*People:* For the gift of love: Lord, hold us so strongly and tenderly in your love that we may have courage to say to those who cross our paths, "You are held in my love; hold me in yours."

*Liturgist:* The Lord did not set his love upon you because you were better than any other people; but the Lord loved you because he elected to love you!

*People:* For the gift of wrath: Lord, teach us that to exercise wrath is to open into the lives of all other human beings the precious gifts of forgiveness and reconciliation.

*Liturgist:* From the heavens you sent wrath;
        the earth feared and was still
    when God arose to establish his wrath
        and to save all the oppressed of the earth.

*People:* For the gift of holiness: Lord pour it out upon us in such measure that we dare take up our humanity and love an unloving world.

*Liturgist:* Thus says the high and lofty One, who inhabits
eternity, whose name is holy, "I dwell in the high and
holy place, and also with him who is of a contrite and
humble heart."

*People:*   Both we and our fathers have forsaken your Way,
O Lord; we have turned aside from your path
and not been faithful.
Yet, you have saved us out of your grace,
and have given into our keeping your
marvelous gifts.

*Liturgist:* If it had not been the Lord who was on our side,
then over us would have gone the raging of the
world.
Blessed be the Lord,
from whom come all good gifts.

*People:* Blessed be the Lord!

*Liturgist:* Blessed be the Lord! Amen!

*People:* Amen!

PART FIVE

# THE HOPE AND SALVATION
# OF COVENANT LIVING

## 29. The Hope of Man Within the Covenant (1)

*Isaiah 9:2-7*

I recall listening once at a General Synod meeting to a Mexican-American migrant worker. In his thick accent he told us of the utter hopelessness of his people in their oppression. He said, "You people come here and you stay in a hotel like this. I have never been in a hotel like this in all my life. I come here and speak to you, and you all wear suits and ties. I never owned a suit and tie." He went on to talk further about the hopelessness of his people. Yet that migrant worker had within his words and within himself a sense that there must be a way out. There had to be some hope. And so the voice of hope and hopelessness was one voice, and from that one voice we heard despair and perhaps some joy.

Hope is the thing we need as much as anything in this world. Teilhard de Chardin says that when mankind ceases to hope it will cease to exist. Hope is that important. Early in the Old Testament the concept of hope centered on a return to paradise, Eden revisited. This was the ultimate goal of God's providence. Both man and nature would return to this initial perfection.

This vision of the early Old Testament has three very important dimensions for us. First is the idea that Israel is the mediator of the gifts of God to the whole world. Israel's goal was to take the gifts of God and hold them up and show the world what they are. Thus Israel was pushing history to its fulfillment. Why is that important for us? I suggest that that remains the essence of the rationale of the church today. The church is to be the demonstrator of the gifts of God. Only if the church holds up to the world an alternate way of life has the world any hope.

The second thing we gain from this Old Testament vision is that the past and the future (these two entities in which we do so much of our living) are one unity in an eternal present. Why is that important for us? It is important for us to realize that it is utterly hopeless to live in the past or to live for the future. Living in the past will only sap our best energy, and living for the future will only misdirect our best resources. Eternal life is life that is lived in the now, because the now is the moment of eternity. Hope has to do not with yesterday, nor with tomorrow. It has only to do with the value of today.

The third thing we learn from the early Old Testament vision is that the destiny of God holds all of our life together. And this is important for us because if we depend only on our own resources, all of life is ultimately hopeless. We must trust a higher law to be moving toward the goal of all creation. It is only in this trust that we dare have any hope. Our own resources do not give us enough upon which to hope.

The great prophets took all of this and built solidly upon this foundation, but they made a very important change. They said that hope does not have to do with a return to paradise, but hope is the establishment of God's Kingdom. The difference between a return to paradise and the establishment of God's Kingdom is this: paradise regained is a return to innocence, and that is futile; but the Kingdom of God established is a maturing to the responsibility of being human. This is the fulfillment of our humanity: not innocence but responsibility. The prophets then, on this basis, added some very important dimensions to the concept of hope.

Hosea saw hope as the untiring and unfailing love of God in our lives. God wants us to depend upon him completely. How we need that hope in our lives. Isaiah said that hope is the victory and the rule of righteousness

and justice in men's lives. Israel was to be the ethical
demonstration of God's justice to all the nations. How the
world needs the church to fulfill that role today. For
Jeremiah, hope was the divine love in the heart of every
man. He said that there would be no barriers of race or
class or nationhood among mankind. We would all be one
family of God. Sometimes I feel optimistic enough to
think that I can see that hope growing in our world.
Ezekiel saw hope as the birth of peace in each person and
in all mankind so that everywhere the Spirit of God would
be accepted as the indwelling presence of being. Isaiah said
that hope would be harmony among all the nations. There
would be a spirit of justice that could not be destroyed by
any worldly power. Love and justice, peace and brotherhood—these are the new dimensions that the prophets
brought to the understanding of hope.

The important thing about these is that they represent
in no way a return to an infantile innocence. Justice and
love and peace—these represent the nobility of the human
creature in its most glorious maturity.

For the prophets the figure of a Savior was crucial to all
of this. He would be one who would come and execute
righteousness and justice for the afflicted and the troubled,
one who would bring aid to the oppressed and the downtrodden, one who would reconcile the alienated and the
warring. This Savior, in the minds of the prophets, would
bring a new social order.

This is very crucial for us to remember. The prophets
were not talking about a new religious order; they really
were not very interested in that. The Savior would bring a
new social order. He would destroy individualism. Lust for
gain in our personal life would not be tolerated. Each man
would live only to provide love for his brother. And the
Savior would destroy all lust for power within every
nation. Each people would have as its goal only the lifting
up of every other people. This was the great vision of the
ultimate destiny of our humanity that the prophets gave to
us, and it is a great gift.

But it did not happen. As justice and love and peace failed to materialize, the concept of hope in our faith gradually changed. It seemed that these great values would not be realized in the world in which men lived, and so hope was spiritualized. Men began to direct their hope beyond the life of this world in a heaven beyond this existence, a place where all of earthly burdens would be released and we would live in a blissful kind of situation. Up to this point hope had been the conquest of this life and this world through justice and love and peace exercised to each other; now hope focused on the conquest of death through resurrection.

This is a very subtle shift, but one with far-reaching implications. As soon as hope no longer has room for the conquest of this life through justice and peace and love, we can tolerate oppression and hatred and war. We can kill our brothers and call it a "just war," because we can hope that we will be forgiven when we die. We can do all manner of things in this life, and as long as we can rationalize them we can hope that we will get away with them because we will be forgiven when we die. All of this will be solved after death. Individualism can be tolerated. We can lust after gain in our own life and not worry too much about loving our brother because we may be forgiven then. And nationalism can be tolerated—the just war. The struggle of this world is replaced by the idea of a glorious repose in heaven. There is no need any more to fight and to struggle to remove evil from the world. One can sit back and wait it out in the anticipation that there is going to be a better situation. And eternity has been shifted from the *now* to the *then*, from the *here* to the *there*, from this moment of *my life* to something that may happen after *my death*. This created in people a paralyzing inability to act. It caused men to be satisfied with the status quo. Why change things? It will all be changed *then* and *there*. Israel lost hope. The people of the Old Testament became a hopeless people. I would suggest that perhaps today this is one of the great sicknesses of the churches. We have lost hope. We have become a hopeless people.

But when God's people become hopeless, hope has to be restored. Two things must be kept in tension: first, that justice and love and peace are the critical business of man's living now; and second, that if man chooses that life style now, death will never destroy the value of his life. The now and the then.

So there burst on this world one who shattered all the hopelessness of man. Suddenly once again the world had to contend with one who was determined to restore hope. That was Jesus, of course. Here was one who once again would join the struggle and the fight against evil. Here was one who would not tolerate the status quo with its rampant individualism and nationalism. His whole life was a living out of his utter opposition to such categories. Here was one who would act now and not await some heavenly reward. Jesus was the synthesis of all of man's desperate attempts to hope. His whole life was one consistent demonstration of justice and love and peace exercised to the people around him. Thus Jesus fulfilled all the expectations of the prophets as the Savior. He was the realization of the Kingdom of God right here on earth among people. And as you well know, his was no easy return to innocence, but a struggling forward toward responsible maturity. Jesus was not born mature. He struggled and worked and toiled to reach maturity. Jesus achieved the ultimate goal of being human, and he returned eternity from the then and the there to the now and the here. He held all of life together because he believed in the destiny of God, and he believed it was happening to him in this moment. Jesus became the hope of all mankind, and that is why we call him the Christ.

When we as Christians are asked how we define hope, we say: Jesus the Christ! There is no philosophy nor even a theology of hope. In Jesus hope is reborn. Hope is not life after death. Hope is not the accomplishments of the past or the pretensions of the future. Hope is the eternal life of justice and peace and love lived out in the now. That is the hope that is laid upon us as Christians—to take hold of the eternal life that is available to us now if we are willing to live by justice and peace and love.

## 30. The Hope of Man Within the Covenant (2)

*Isaiah 11*

In the last sermon we sought to discover the dimensions of what it means for man to hope, to look beyond the existential despair in which he finds himself and toward those things which make life beautiful and meaningful. Hope—that is our theme. We said that hope should not be seen as a return to the innocence of Eden but rather as a maturing toward responsible humanness that fulfills the Kingdom of God. We said that hope should not be seen as the conquest of death through resurrection leading to eternal bliss in Heaven, but as the conquest of this world and this life through justice and love and peace, which creates in our lives an eternal now.

Granting all of this, what does that mean for us in our times? I would like to approach this in three ways: First, what does hope mean for the Christian church today? Second, what does hope mean for the Christian person today? And third, what does hope mean for God's world today?

Let us begin with the Christian church. How does the Christian church hope in this world in which we live? I want to share with you at this time some of my own thoughts about the church in this age. You may radically disagree with what I am going to project. As someone who has tried to make a study of this situation, looking at the past and trying to project it into where we are now and what the future holds, these are some of the conclusions I have drawn.

I believe that we are entering upon an age of radical unbelief. As I look over the past, I think back on the Middle Ages, the great period of medieval history. This is often called the Age of Faith. Will Durant in his monumental study of history has a huge volume that deals with the medieval period, which he entitles *The Age of Faith.* I would like to take issue with that. I think that this was in fact not an age of "Christian faith," although it certainly was an age of feudal religiosity. What happened during that time was that the social and cultural system used institutional religion for its own ends and vice versa. The *faith* was held in those small enclaves of people who made up the monasteries. The great reforms of Cluny, the Cistercians, St. Francis, and St. Dominic kept the light of faith burning. The Christian faith during the Middle Ages was not kept in the culture, but in the very small, rather isolated groups of Christians who were affected by the monastic reforms.

The Reformation burst onto the human scene at a time when it would seem that in God's providence the world was in desperate need of Christian hope. It was a time almost like the time of Jesus, when in the providence of God the world was ready. In the sixteenth century, apparently, the world was once again receptive and the Word came. The Word came from the monks—Erasmus, Luther, and Calvin were all trained in the monastery. Although the period that followed the Reformation has been called the Age of Enlightenment or the Age of Reason, that does not necessarily dissociate it from Christian faith. I would suggest that the four hundred years since the Reformation have been throughout the world (not in small enclaves of people, but on a much broader scale) an Age of Faith, an age when the faith has spread far and wide. Especially has this been true through the great missionary endeavors of the last century.

But I suggest we have come to an end. I believe we have had four hundred years in which the faith has spread as a very potent and dynamic force within the world of men

—shaping the great democracies; giving birth to the great humanitarian movements; being within the culture of man the great adjustor of social injustice. Certainly there has been a great deal of injustice done in the name of the faith; but probably, as much as at any time in Christian history, during these last four hundred years the Christian faith has also sought to adjust those injustices. It has been a time of faith and it is at an end.

What does this mean for the church? Shall we give up in despair and say we have reached a hopeless situation? Isaiah did not do that in the face of Assyria. Isaiah looked for the time when, in God's providence, the Word would once again be needed and heard. And that, I believe, is the Word of God to the church today. The time will come again. I make no speculation as to how soon: it may be one hundred years; it may be four hundred years; it may be seven hundred years. In feudal Europe it was close to twelve hundred years. But the day will come again when, in the providence of God, it will once again be time for the hope of the faith.

What am I saying? I am saying that as I look to the future, what I see needed in the church today is a "new monasticism." I am not suggesting that we all go off and become monks or nuns somewhere. Far from it! I am saying that one of the essential qualities of monasticism was that it provided a small enclave of people who together in covenant—and that is what the discipline of the monastery was, a covenant—held the faith in the world. They did not let the light go out. They held that faith by practicing what was called, in monastic jargon, hospitality. Their intention was to practice justice, and love, and peace among themselves and toward the world outside. Thus the world would have an opportunity to see an alternative way of life. That is the way the best reformed monks lived, practicing justice, love, and peace to the world around them and to each other.

This, I would suggest to you, gives a clue to the future of the parish church. It must become a small enclave of covenanted people who realize that they no longer represent the culture or society in which they live, who realize that they have stepped apart, not from seeking to do justice, love, and peace—they will still practice these in the world—but for the purpose of demonstrating an alternative way of life to what the world is currently practicing. And those small enclaves of people will provide for the world what we might call a "new monasticism." The number of Christians will be radically reduced. There will be no more sociological Christianity, no more members on the rolls of the churches because it is the cultural thing to do. As the numbers go down, the commitment to Christianity will rise spectacularly, because Christianity will no longer be made lukewarm by lukewarm people within the churches. To be a Christian will mean to be a covenanted person who stands over against the way of the world, offering an alternative way of life. As commitment increases spectacularly (the kind of commitment there was in the early church and the kind of commitment that was stimulated by the reformers), the churches will begin seriously, patiently, and unceasingly to do justice and love and peace within the fellowship of the church and toward the world outside the church. The churches will again begin to practice, in utter seriousness and commitment, *hospitality*. The churches will keep the light burning through the next centuries of unbelief until mankind is ready to believe again.

I do not see this situation as hopeless or as full of despair. I see it as creating the eternal now by conquering the world through showing it an alternate way of life. I see all of this as the hope of the church.

What does this mean for each of us as Christian persons? I suggest that the future of God's goal and of man's destiny depends radically (as it does only occasionally in history) on the level of commitment of each Christian. In the history of mankind there are only rare moments that God gives when the level of each person's commitment becomes totally crucial. It was that crucial in the monasteries of the Middle Ages. It will now become that crucial in the churches of the next few centuries. Our commitment must be maximum. There will be no room for uncommitted people. Our faithfulness must be maximum. There will be nothing for the semifaithful man to do in the church. He can do it all better in the world. We must be determined to demonstrate patiently in our own lives the meanings of justice and love and peace. We must be determined to demonstrate *hospitality*, an alternate way of life in a chaotic world.

Where shall we get the resources to do this? How can we, poor, beggarly, unfaithful, uncommitted people, do this? I really believe, Christians, that as seldom before in history God is ready to pour his grace out upon us. There is the problem. *We simply do not believe* that God is that ready to give us that much grace. He will not call us to more than we are able to do, nor will he fail to give us strength for that to which he calls us. There is where we are. He will call us and give us the strength if we will open ourselves and be receptive. The problem we are facing in our tepid churches is that we do not believe it.

I am reminded of the remark of Walt Kelly's cartoon character Pogo: "We have met the enemy and they are *us.*" That is our problem. We have met the enemy and they are us, because we really do not believe that God is that gracious. We really do not believe he will give us that much power. But he will! These are the times when God gives power, and these are the times when faithful and committed people open themselves to receive it. That is our hope. God's grace is available to us, waiting to be poured out upon us to make us each a strong, committed, faithful brother of Jesus the Christ, ready to do justice and peace and love in this world. What we must do is quit being our own enemies. That is our hope.

What does all this mean for the world? I believe that mankind is initiating vast new searches for new gods. Man does this from time to time, in order to test whether God is real or not. There is nothing remarkable about that. Let

mankind spend three centuries, a half a millennium searching, but in the end it will peter out. In the end man will
know that he has found no new god. And, Christians,
when that happens, the church that you as committed
and faithful persons have kept burning in the world will
burst into flame—the candle will become the sun. At that
moment the Christian faith must be ready. It will only be
ready insofar as each one of us has taken seriously our
brotherhood to Christ and our responsibility to be Christlike toward our brother.

When the world needs hope again, if we have been
faithful and if the church has been kept in covenant (if
together we and the church have shown hospitality—an
alternate way of life), the hope of the world will once
again, as it always has, reside in the church of God. That is
a fact from the days of our father Abraham. From his time
to ours the hope of the world has been kept in God's
faithful people. When the world is ready to hope again we
will be there! And that is not a question—will we be
there?—but an affirmation. The church will be there with
hope because of the grace of God. We will be there!

## 31. The Salvation of God Within the Covenant (1)

### Ezekiel 37:1-14

*The salvation of God.* What do we, whose lives are ordered by the Puritan ethic and the American dream, mean by that? After all, does salvation not belong to man—especially if he is industrious, efficient, and capable?

There is a heresy rampant within our churches. Its sources lie in Victorian morality, which stresses rugged individualism, and in the social gospel, which affirmed we could cure all of man's ills in our generation. The result of all these is that man understands himself as the author of his own salvation, a salvation which he is quite confident he can hammer out on the anvil of his soul.

There is a Peanuts cartoon by Charles Schulz that is appropriate here, I think. Charlie Brown and Lucy are leaning on their philosopher's wall. Charlie Brown says, "You know what I wonder? Sometimes I wonder if God is pleased with me." He turns to Lucy and says, "Do you ever wonder if God is pleased with you?" And Lucy turns; and with that big wicked smile that she gets on her face, she fluffs her hair a little in the back and retorts, "He just has to be." Think about it. Most of us are quite confident that God just has to be pleased with us, because everything we do is designed to create our own salvation, and if we are creating our salvation how can he turn us down?

We could hardly blame the intelligent human animal for wanting to create his own salvation, because in his intelligence there is always the lurking doubt that maybe God cannot manage it. Are we honest enough really to ask that

179

question: Are we quite confident that God can manage our salvation? Or is there a lurking doubt? I do not know about you, but that lurking doubt is always inside me somewhere. I am never quite sure that God can manage my salvation. Who among us would risk relying totally upon God? It is far more wise to distribute our bets on the chance that the winnings may accrue a little better if we know how to scatter them. Certainly out of the Puritan ethic and the American dream we would not suspect that God could object to a substantial amount of self-reliance.

What do we mean when we talk about the salvation of God? I would like to define it very simply: Salvation is *God's free gift of justice, love, and peace to every person, to the covenant community* (which we know as the church), *and most especially to all mankind.* God's free gift of justice, love, and peace. A life set free from fear and oppression and aimlessness and guilt. The energy by which God releases this gift into the world is what we call *grace.* The result of what happens is a new way of life. Paul called it "a new being." Jesus called it "rebirth." The point is that it is a whole new content, a whole new context through which life is changed. As the "now generation" puts it, we become radicalized—radicalized to justice and love and peace. The theological term for that is "redemption" or "resurrection."

The issue is that man cannot exist out of the harvest of his own resources. It is only as he receives the free gift of God that sets him free to justice and love and peace that he begins to understand what it means to engage in salvation by faith. Like the original life that we were given—and we were given it; not one of us earned the right to be on this earth—this new life directed toward justice and love and peace is the *gift* of God. A man dare not trust his own achievements when he has the opportunity to absorb the energy that God has ready to pour out on him. This is the core of the difference between God's faith and man's religion. In man's religion man is striving through his own achievements; in God's faith he is absorbing the gift that God would give.

The Old Testament prophets understood this subtle nuance well. God's salvation—his justice and his love and his peace—is poured out into history. The eternal will shapes nations and people; it shapes the churches; it shapes the person, your life. Man is not cast adrift on his own resources. He becomes aware that the energy of God is breaking open his life, an energy that cannot be abstracted or intellectualized but only lived with as we live in relation to other people. So God's salvation cannot be spiritualized to some remote heavenly paradise. Salvation is directed to the anguish and the torment and the guilt and the hopelessness of this world. Salvation offers a different way of life in the eternal here and the eternal now. Salvation is the energy of renewal—resurrection, if you will—of the person and the community. Salvation is God's creation of a new humanity that will bring the Kingdom of God. It is not an individual salvation of the soul into a kind of heavenly leisure, but the realization among people on this earth of justice and love and peace.

The Christian affirms that this is an actual possibility in the lives of man. This is not a philosophy. This is not a never-never-land fairy tale. This happened. And it happened in the person of Jesus. Just so, it can happen in the person of any one of us. Jesus was the living demonstration of justice and love and peace. He was salvation incarnate. The Christian faith declares that that option is open to every human being.

The interesting thing is that Jesus' life was not a miracle. Some people say, "We cannot possibly emulate his life; we cannot possibly be like that. Jesus' life was a miracle." But that is not so. Jesus' life was the natural way life is intended to be lived. Justice and love and peace—that is not miraculous; that is natural. If a miracle is the interruption of the natural by the unnatural, then the miracle is rather that there are men who refuse the option, that there are men who refuse to live the natural kind of life that Jesus calls them to live—justice and peace and love. And what a dreadful, awful miracle that is.

This means that God's salvation is earthly. It is ethical and concrete. The gift determines how men are going to relate to each other. This does not mean that it conforms to or supports things the way they are now. Christians are often somewhat confused at this point. The Christian faith affirms that God's creation is good. It does not affirm that the status quo is good. And yet there are countless churchmen who live out of the latter supposition. The Christian faith affirms that the Christian is called to take a responsible place in the world. It does not affirm that the Christian is called to reflect the world around him. Yet there are many churchmen who live out of the latter supposition. The Christian faith affirms that the church's mission is to be a servant to the world of men. It does not affirm that the church's mission is to bless the things the world does. Yet there are countless churchmen who live out of the latter supposition. On the other hand, there are countless firm, devout Christians who live out of those former suppositions: that God's creation is good, that the Christian's responsibility is to take his place within it, and that the church's mission is to be a servant.

What this means, then, is that God's salvation has dimensions that are far beyond this world. The new order of the Kingdom of God will be different from the present one. This is radically clear in the life of Jesus. The crucifixion (which represents this world) and the resurrection (which represents the new world) set this in sharp relief. It also means that God's energy is more potent than men's aspirations. Again, the crucifixion and the resurrection set this in sharp and dramatic relief. The salvation of God (justice, love, and peace) will ultimately prevail. Man can make a hash of life, but God's intention will go relentlessly forward. And it is here that we find our best hope and our eternal joy. We can make an awful mess of our lives, but God will raise out of that his Kingdom. That is resurrection. We can make a mess of the churches, and God will raise out of that his Kingdom. That is resurrection. We can make an awful mess of this world in which we live, but there is confidence and hope that God will raise out of our worst messes his Kingdom. And he is doing that. You can see signs of it if you look. That is resurrection.

This means that we must see the destiny of our own lives and of our churches in much larger terms. Salvation is not just for us and for our churches. Salvation is God's act for all creation, and we are simply the instruments through which he elects to do this. The church is called to hold up the light of justice and love and peace so the world can see it, and every Christian person is called to be as the Messiah to the person next to him. Are we ready to take up that calling? Our election is to stand against oppression and hatred and war and for justice and love and peace. When we do that, we are prophesying. We are saying to the dry bones, "Life will come upon you." This kind of prophetic living allows no room for pride or privilege, but it lays on us the burdens and the joys of responsible service. It causes us to see our lives and our times in both humility and also in the greatest of nobility.

That is why the faithful Christian begins every week and every day with the celebration of God's saving acts. Celebration is the fine tuning of our actions to the mighty saving power of God. Without celebration our real understanding of our prophetic role—our real understanding of what it means to do justice and love and peace—goes out of focus. But when, in the act of adoring celebration, we open ourselves to receive into our being the free gifts of God—salvation and justice and love and peace—all the dry bones of our souls' most deserted valleys will knit together again; all the sinews and flesh and skin will come upon us and renew our comeliness as God's created beings. The breath of the Almighty will be the power of our words and our deeds. Then at last we shall stand on our feet in maturity and responsibility, and for the first time will live. And the whole world will rejoice, because it will see the salvation of God in the lives of men who live by justice and by love and by peace. That salvation is the hope of the world. The Lord God says to you, "Son of man, daughter of man, prophesy!" Justice. Love. Peace. Prophesy!

## 32. The Salvation of God Within the Covenant (2)

### Ezekiel 37:1-14

For several centuries now everything has been closing up on the first day of the week. The reason for this has been to celebrate God's achievement. Why do we gather in churches on Sunday? We gather to celebrate what God does: his salvation. That is why things are closed on Sunday; that is why we celebrate.

In the preceding sermon we defined salvation as the free gift of God's justice and love and peace delivered to the person, the church, and all mankind. We said this salvation was actualized in the life of Jesus the Christ. The crucifixion is the symbol of the world's hopeless despair, torn by oppression and hatred and war. The resurrection is the symbol of the world's eternal hope in God's saving grace of justice and love and peace. We also said that this salvation can be realized in our lives and our times. God directs his salvation to our specific needs as persons and the church and the whole world. Thus hope and salvation come together when the healing of God meets the hurt of man. This occurs not by the striving of man, not by the achieving of human beings, but by the free grace of God. Thus human hope finds fulfillment in trust in God's salvation.

The people of the Old Testament had fantastic trust in the saving power of God to realize his destiny. The whole concept of the *holy people* is founded on the hope and trust of God's salvation, not of man's activity. This was honed to a razor keenness by the words of the prophets; and it becomes strikingly clear in Ezekiel with his vision of the dry bones. Man's hope finds fulfillment in God's saving acts. God raises up the Hebrew nation out of the grave. God gives the flesh and the breath and the life. But the critical point, which we so often miss, is that God does it in his own time. Why did those dry bones lie there so long? Why was Israel left in her grave so long? Why was not someone summoned earlier to prophesy? Why did not God's saving grace come more quickly? The answer of the people of the Old Testament was that destiny evolves at its own speed. They called this the "fulness of time." And the Hebrews had absolute trust in the fulness of time.

This is the main directive of the lives of the apostles in the New Testament. In Jesus God fulfills his destiny, but he does it in his own good time. Jesus' whole life is a disaster: he is laid in the grave; he is nothing more than dry bones! And yet in the fulness of time God renews his life and purpose. It is small wonder that the early Christians exhibited trust and hope and patience. They were witnesses to the saving acts of God in the fulness of time. This did not mean that they lost their social conscience; but it did mean they were able to hold an expansive view of God's salvation. Why did Jesus not come earlier? The question was simply answered: Because in the ongoing march of the human race *this* was the time of God's gracious act. And from this, man can learn to trust that God will relentlessly work his destiny.

But trusting in God is an immeasurably difficult thing. It involves utter faith and an expansive perspective: hope and trust and patience. From these apostolic understandings of the fulness of time the early Church Fathers quickly departed. The Church Fathers began to place importance upon the works of man for salvation. Worship, sacraments, almsgiving, and prayers became the means of salvation. Faith was no longer trust and hope and patience, but belief in the doctrines of the church. After many centuries of this, the Reformers rediscovered the meaning of faith. Once again they put hope and trust and patience into the content of faith—the assurance of the saving grace of God in the fulness of time. Then came along the Puritan ethic, and our forbears tied *trust* to *vocation*. Once again salvation by the works of man became predominant. Trust in yourself. Hope in your own ability. Achieve. It is out of this kind of ethic that our whole culture has been put together; and today we are still in the grip of this Puritan insight (or lack of insight, if you will; or heresy, if you must).

Think of our situation as persons: caught in the externalization of life; taught to achieve goals but never told why; directed outwardly before we have achieved any stabilization inwardly. Our worth is adjudged by how busy we are (and that is a good way of avoiding having to live with ourselves); our compassion by how many causes we support. We know the world so well, and we are so unacquainted with ourselves. It is salvation by works, Christians, and most of our lives are afflicted by this dread paralysis. Most of the people I meet have lives that are marked by hopelessness, by lack of trust, and by an awful impatience. Their lives are valleys of dry bones. They have been laid in their graves while they are yet walking about.

I suggest that there is only one alternative: to return to the salvation of God. This does not involve the loss of human concern for the needs of others. It does involve an inner renewal and a new perspective. It involves trust and hope and patience (and patience is never indifference). It involves a willingness to live in the fulness of time. It involves the risk of being willing to rely on the fact that the God who was at work in Jesus Christ will be at work in us. And then we will fulfill what we were created for: that is, to be as Messiahs to each other. This will increase our sensitivity to the needs of others. This is the salvation of God in our personal lives—trust, hope, patience, inner renewal. The other alternative is the grave while living—dry bones.

The churches are afflicted with the same dreadful paralysis that afflicts most people. During the great evangelical awakening of the eighteenth century all men were going to be converted. It did not happen. The goal of the great mission enterprise of the nineteenth century was that the world would be won for Christ within the century. It did not happen. The social gospel of the twentieth century was meant to rebuild the world, not in our century, but in our generation. It has not happened. For three hundred years the churches have been subjected to fantastic expenditures of frenetic energy. And the world is more hostile to the churches than ever before, and the churches are better sensitized to the needs of the world than ever before. But the churches, in being so well acquainted with the world, have remained unacquainted with their Lord. So churches today are marked by growing frustration (an indication of their hopelessness), by increasing activism (an indication of their lack of trust), and by a fearful sense of irrelevancy (an indication of their impatience).

Today the churches are dry bones scattered upon the desert floor. I believe that only one alternative remains: we must return as Christian communities to the salvation of God. This does not involve a loss of social conscience; it involves the gaining of a new perspective. The churches today must learn to rely in patience upon God's relentless workings. The churches today must learn salvation. They must learn what it means to do justice and love and peace without impatience. Then they will be what God created them to be: Messiahs to the world. The alternative to this is death for the churches.

The world is caught in the same paralyzing disaster. Consumed with attempts to save itself (and there is no need to rehearse them), it is no different from what it has always been. Some of these attempts are good and some are not so good. But there is no hope and no trust and no patience and no sense of purpose in the world in which we live. It is a valley of dry bones. And so the world asks: Who will prophesy an alternative way of life? Who will renew this world with purpose? Is there a way out?

The Christian affirmation is: Yes, there is a way. We believe with all our hearts that God created this world good; and he is not about to lose it now. So Christians—as persons and as the corporate church—provide the alternative. There is a goal toward which things are moving. There is a fulness of time in which these things occur. You may call it providence. You may call it destiny. It is the realization of justice and love and peace. It is the salvation of God.

There is a song by Paul Simon in which these words are sung: "Slow down; you move too fast; you got to make the mornin' last." The church and the Christians in it must hear these words too: Slow down; you are going too fast; you will not save the world until you know the power of God's salvation in your life. And the church will not save the world until it knows the power of God's salvation within it. We must learn how to accept as well as do justice and love and peace. This, I suggest to you, is a vision of *eternal optimism*, for it takes seriously the whole concept of the fulness of time. Life is based not on man's achievements, but on God's salvation.

There is a hymn we sing: "God the Omnipotent!/King, who ordainest/Thunder thy clarion,/the lightning thy sword;/Show forth thy pity on/high where thou reignest/; *Give to us peace in our time, O Lord.*" But note how the last stanza ends: "*Thou wilt* give peace *in thy time,* O Lord." This does not mean that man does not search to discover peace and love and justice. It means that in the midst of that search he recognizes that the ultimate, final destiny belongs to God. When we can truly couple "Give to us peace in our time, O Lord" with "Thou wilt give peace in thy time, O Lord"—when we can put those two together and live out of that context, the salvation of God is mightily upon us.

## 33. The Fulfillment of Hope and Salvation

### Job 30:16-31; 38:1-27; 42:1-6

One of the great American preachers, Jonathan Edwards, once preached a famous sermon called, "Sinners in the Hands of an Angry God." In it he likened man's situation to that of a spider being held on a web over the eternal flames of hell.

That does not strike us much any more; but in Edwards' day, given the theology with which his people were familiar, that said a great deal about the existential situation of man and a great deal about the destiny of God. For the human being hangs suspended on a gossamer thread between the void of the before and the void of the beyond; between an unknown origin and an uncertain future; between the unremembered and the unremembering. How slender that thread is! This little life of ours—these few days, this short time—compasses us about with terrifying limitations. Is life nothing more than existential despair, or is it filled with eternal destiny?

The faith that we profess as Christians takes both sides of this question in utter seriousness. The essence of our affirmation is that man lives life within the existential situation, but that the life man lives has an eternal context. Despair and destiny are recognized as the twin tensions of our existence. This affirmation is articulated in two ways: first, through the Word of God given to us in the Scriptures, and especially as we discover it lived out in the lives of the people of the Old Testament. And second, in the Word of God as given to us in the life of the man Jesus who is called the Christ. The content of that single Word has four cornerstones: salvation and grace, covenant and hope.

*Salvation.* God—what is he? What else but the creative energy behind and within and before everything that exists; creating all things from the hydrogen atom to the virus to the stone to the tree; creating creatures, the most sophisticated of which is man who achieves his sophistication through intellect and freedom and will. The essence of this creative energy is what we call love.

Love is the power of the universe that draws all that exists into a cohesive unity, the power that makes all things hang together. It is a power that is exemplified in two laws: the Law of Continuance (which we call evolution) and the Law of Cohesion (which we call unity). These laws of love seek two goals. The first goal is personalness. Each person in the whole world should have the opportunity to define the maximum dimensions of his humanity. That is called justice. The second goal is corporateness. In discovering our personhood we discover how to live together in harmony. That is called peace.

Thus we live in a world that is moving into the future. Mankind is evolving. We live in a world that is moving toward cohesion. Unification is happening. We live in a world that is being personalized. Justice is coming. We live in a world that is being communalized. We are learning how to live together in peace. All of this affirms that the context of the life in which we are set is the context of an eternal destiny. And yet, at the same time, that future is always uncertain. There is always the danger that union will become exploitation, that personalization will become individualism, and that community will become oppression.

Suddenly we discover ourselves once again in the middle of the existential situation: a situation in which a decision is being demanded of us to accept or reject the salvation of God.

*Grace.* We are not left helpless as we face that decision.

Our lives are energized by the power of God's gracious gifts—personhood, spirituality, steadfastness, wrath, righteousness, love, holiness, and all the rest. These are the powerful gifts that arm us to make a decision for God. We can decide that the context of our lives will be justice and peace. We are given the power to appropriate the grace of God's salvation poured out upon us.

Yet, we must always remember that this is a free gift of God, a free act. We do absolutely nothing to merit it. There is nothing in our existence that says God has to give it to us; we cannot win it by our striving. We are simply dependent upon the grace of God who gives it into life. Thus the context of life is again set in the perspective of eternal destiny.

It is at this point that we recognize our freedom to refuse the gift. Grace can be rejected! Our freedom crashes down upon us as an awesome burden. Our lives are suddenly staggered back into existential despair. The potential of our personal freedom crushes us. We shrink in terror at this kind of awesome responsibility. We can choose. Overcome with panic, the panic of desolation, many of us become isolated and lonely. Fear grips us, and we are dashed upon the rock of our own freedom.

*Covenant.* We are spared from going forward into that kind of situation alone and isolated and terrified. There are other human beings with whom to share this life, who face the same decision and the same grace and the same terror. And there is a man, Jesus, who has faced the same decision and the same grace and the same terror. Suddenly we become aware of the fact that we are in relation to all other human beings and to this man Jesus whom we call the Christ.

Now all of life is understood as an intricate weaving of the webs of interpersonal relationship. Nothing happens in a vacuum, but everything is actions and attitudes that are responses to actions and attitudes. We are not abandoned or damned to isolation. Slowly and painfully we begin to learn that we can live out these relationships in gratitude.

We can be grateful for other human beings and for Jesus called the Christ. Then all of life suddenly begins to take on a different kind of aura. It becomes a celebration. All of life becomes worship, a festival of the gifts of God, an adoration of his salvation.

We are constantly forming and re-forming the covenants that we make with those about us as we live within this intricately woven web of interaction. Living becomes an adventure and an exploration of new covenants. So once again the context of life is set in eternal destiny.

And yet covenants are very fragile things. Those whom we have so soon learned to trust betray us; like Job's friends, like Judas. Our noblest aspirations turn into dust and ashes, and we feel diseased like Job or crucified like Jesus. The power of love seems to slip through the fingers of our souls like so much divine sand. Before us rises again the phoenix of existential despair. The bright sun of our destiny is eclipsed in the dark shadow of despair. The waves of terror and guilt break over us, dragging us back down into the undertow. As we gasp and flail about we are sure that at last we are undone.

*Hope.* Here is the one thing that existential despair cannot touch. Despair can blur our understanding of the salvation of God and make us insecure about the outpouring of his gifts. It can shake the foundations of our relationship with our brothers and our Christ. But the one thing despair cannot do is reduce hope to dust and ashes. When salvation and the gifts of God and the covenant have seemingly all been taken away from us, when we in our poverty feel we have nothing spiritual left, there is one possession, and that possession is hope. It is no whistling in the dark. It is the assurance that we can live by justice and peace, that we can lay hold again on the gifts of God, the assurance that his grace is still there, that we can find new and renewed relationships with our brothers and our Christ, that once again life will be lived as gratitude.

This means that hope stands not over against despair, but that hope stands in the midst of despair. It defines the eternal destiny inside the existential situation. Hope is what transforms the hominoid animal into the human being. Our humanness, Christians, is not defined by intelligence, or by reason, or by speech, or by any of the other things by which we are wont to define it. Our humanness is defined by the ability to reflect upon the eternal context inside the present situation: the ability to comprehend destiny in the midst of our despair.

It is hope that makes us once again bearers of God's salvation and his gifts and his covenant. It transforms our little lives into a larger love and thereby heightens our personhood while at the same time submerging our individual selfishness. Hope is that quality of faith into which despair cannot reach.

Salvation, grace, covenant, hope. That is the Word of God revealed in the lives of the people of the Old Testament. That is also the Word of God revealed in the life of that man Jesus whom we call the Christ. If we were to sum up the Word of God—salvation, grace, covenant, and hope—the summary would be *Jesus*. It is this Word that resolves the tension between our existential despair and the eternal destiny. Both are the realities of life and faith. The one defines the situation of life. We read it when we rehearse the faith we believe: ". . . he has come to us and shared our common lot." That is the situation of life. The other defines the context of life. We read it when we rehearse the faith: ". . . conquering sin and death and reconciling the world to himself." Despair: ". . . he shared our common lot." Destiny: " . . . reconciling the world to himself." Here all the hurt of man meets and is met by the mighty healing of God.

That is the faith in its essence. That is the faith we discover in the lives of the people of the Old Testament. That is the faith we discover in the life of Jesus, and that is why we call him the Christ. That is the faith we hold by the grace of God.

# A Daily Office for Covenant Life

*Lift up your heart.*
I lift it up unto the Lord.

## CONFESSION

*We are called to confess our sins unto God with penitent and contrite hearts:*

MORNING: O God, who ever renews the man who has missed your Way, I come again seeking nobler life in you. I lay upon you this day my deep concern over my own interests; my thoughtlessness of others; my needless anxieties and fruitless fears; my hesitancy in the face of your call to love; my clinging to distrust; my blind confidence in false gods; my want of faith; and my lack of love. Pardon my sins: those I do knowingly, those I do unwittingly, and those I dare not name. Then lead me into a new life with my Elder Brother, Jesus the Christ. Amen.

EVENING: Merciful God: I confess that I have sinned against you in thought and word and deed; that I have not loved you with all my heart and soul, with all my mind and strength; and that I have not loved my neighbors and enemies as I love my self. I beseech you, O God, to be forgiving to what I have been, to help me to amend what I am, and of your great mercy to direct what I shall be; so that the love of goodness may ever be first in my heart, that I may walk in your Way of Love in deep compassion, and return again unto Jesus the Christ. Amen.

*HERE MAY BE: A Hymn, Psalm, etc.*

## *PRAISE*

*Our God has richly blessed us with his gracious gifts; let us rejoice and be glad:*

*MORNING:* Eternal Mystery, whose never failing providence orders all things, I praise you, I glorify you, I give thanks unto you for all you are to me, and all you do for me day by day. For reason and insight; for direction and guidance; for the gifts of the world and the faith; for your patience with me; for your mercy and grace toward me; for my past lived and my future yet to be lived; for the present moment and its possibilities; for these and all other mercies, known or unknown, remembered and forgotten, I praise you now and forever. Amen.

*EVENING:* Gracious God, whose mercies never fail, who is the giver of all the bounty of this life: I thank you for my creation in your image; for your preserving mercy through all the days of my life; for the protection and comfort you give me in the times of my distress; for those whom I love and who love me; for your close concern in my sickness; for your steadfast love in my sorrow; for your glory in my times of joy. I thank you for the daily tasks you have set me to do, and for the strength of will to do them. And above all I thank you for the coming of our Lord into the world; for the gracious words he spoke; for the compassionate work he did; for his bitter passion and atoning sacrifice; and for his mighty resurrection from the dead. I am deeply and humbly grateful that he has offered me pardon for my sins; shown me the means of grace; and given me the indwelling of his Holy Spirit. Amen.

*HERE MAY BE: A Scripture Reading.*

## THE STORY OF THE FAITH

*MORNING:* We believe in one God, the Father, the Almighty, maker of heaven and earth, of all things visible and invisible. We believe in the one Lord, Jesus Christ, the only-begotten Son of God, Son of the Father from all eternity, God from God, Light from Light, true God from true God, begotten, not made, one in being with the Father. Through him all things were made. For us men and for our salvation he came from heaven; by the power of the Holy Spirit he was born of the Virgin Mary, and became man. For our sake he was crucified under Pontius Pilate; he suffered, died, and was buried. He arose on the third day in fulfillment of the Scriptures. He entered into heaven and is seated at the right hand of the Father. He will come again in glory to judge the living and the dead, and his Kingdom will have no end. We believe in the Holy Spirit, the Lord, the giver of life; he proceeds from the Father (and the Son). Together with the Father and the Son he is worshipped and glorified. He has spoken through the prophets. We believe in one, holy, catholic, and apostolic church. We acknowledge one baptism for the forgiveness of sins, we look for the resurrection of the dead, and the life of the world to come. Amen.

*EVENING:* I believe in God, the Eternal Spirit, Father of our Lord Jesus Christ and our Father, and to his deeds I testify. He calls the world into being, creates man in his own image, and sets before him the ways of life and death. He seeks in holy love to save all people from aimlessness and sin. He judges men and nations by his righteous will declared through prophets and apostles. In Jesus Christ, the man of Nazareth, our crucified and risen Lord, he has come to us, and shared our common lot, conquering sin and death, and reconciling the world to himself. He bestows upon us his Holy Spirit, creating and renewing the church of Jesus Christ, binding in covenant faithful people of all ages, tongues, and races.

He calls us into his church: to accept the cost and joy of his discipleship; to be his servants in the service of man; to proclaim the gospel to all the world, and resist the powers of evil; to share in Christ's baptism and eat at his table; to join him in his passion and victory. He promises to all who trust him: forgiveness of sins and fulness of grace; courage in the struggle for justice and peace; his presence in trial and rejoicing; and eternal life in his Kingdom which has no end. Blessing and honor, glory and power be unto him. Amen.

## PETITION

*Our needs as God's children are deep and abiding: let us stand present to God in profound humility:*

*MORNING:* O Lord, make me an instrument of your peace: that where there is hatred I may bring love; that where there is wrong I may bring the spirit of forgiveness; that where there is discord I may bring harmony; that where there is error I may bring hope; that where there is darkness I may bring light; that where there is sadness I may bring joy. Lord, grant that I may seek rather to comfort than to be comforted; to understand rather than to understood; to love rather than to be loved. For it is in giving that one receives; it is in self-forgetting that one finds; it is in forgiving that one is forgiven; it is by dying that one awakens to eternal life. Hear this prayer, O Lord, and grant me your salvation. Amen.

*EVENING:* Lord, our God: I offer and present unto you myself, to be a reasonable, holy, and living sacrifice. Take me as I am and make me more fit for your service. Use me for your Way of Love and make of me a servant of mankind. I am not my own, but yours. Therefore, claim me as your child, keep me as your charge, use me as you will and when you will. And grant that my life may be lived to the glory of your Way and the good of my fellow men. Amen.

## INTERCESSION

*Let us extend our lives to touch the lives of others:*

*MORNING:* Eternal God, the Creator, Redeemer, and Sustainer of all mankind, I pray for all sorts and conditions of men:

That you will give to mankind the gifts of Christ: joy and freedom and simplicity that will make our tired world inspired again; commitment and vision and singlemindedness that will renew a weary humanity;

That you will so reveal yourself in fellowship with men that a world which exists by competition may learn that its survival is dependent upon cooperation;

That you will consecrate the discontent of the young, the rebellious, the prophetic, so that through them may come justice, brotherhood, and the dignity of all mankind.

That you will relieve and succor those weak in body and mind; those who are confused by a changing world; those who are dying, and those who must give them strength and aid;

That you will shower your great love on all who feel themselves outcast, alienated, disenfranchised, imprisoned, lonely, or forgotten,

So that all men may be given a full measure of the humanness flowing from their Elder Brother, Jesus the Christ. Amen.

*EVENING:* O Lord, who calls into being a people consecrated to the holy office of being shepherd for the world and servant for mankind, I pray:

That you will give your church such power that she may have life in its full abundance, with courage to go forward daringly into the unknown future, unfettered by the past;

That you will so inspire and change human nature that all the diminishing manifestations of the Old Age may pass away, and that the glorious possibilities of Christ's New Age may become real in human relationships;

That you will hasten that time in the long progress of man
which you have promised, when all shall be subject to
your hope and joy, and your Kingdom shall be established in power upon this earth,
So that we all may come to the unity of the faith and the
knowledge of Jesus the Christ, gaining full humanness
through a complete measure of the Spirit of our Lord.
Amen.

*HERE MAY BE: the Thanksgiving of Holy Communion.*

*We are bound in covenant love to God our Father, to our
Lord Jesus Christ, and to one another. Let us testify to
this reconciling grace:*

*THE LORD'S PRAYER* (Using "sins")

Our Father in heaven: holy be your name, your Kingdom
come, your will be done, on earth as in heaven. Give us
today our daily bread. Forgive us our sins, as we forgive
those who sin against us. Save us in the time of trial, and
deliver us from evil. For yours is the Kingdom, the power,
and the glory forever. Amen.